MARCO POLO

GW00370453

MENORCA

FRANCE

SWITZER-
LAND

Bilbao

ITALY

ANDORRA   MC

Madrid   Barcelona   Corsica
SPAIN   (F)

Menorca

Valencia   Mallorca

Balearic Islands   Sardinia
                                (I)

Mediterranean
Sea
ALGERIA

www.marco-polo.com

FREE!

THE
TOURING APP

shows you the way...
including routes and offline maps!

GET MORE OUT OF YOUR MARCO POLO GUIDE

IT'S AS SIMPLE AS THIS

1 go.marco-polo.com/men

2 download and discover

GO!

WORKS OFFLINE!

SYMBOLS

 Insider Tip

★ Highlight

●●●● Best of...

☼ Scenic view

♲ Responsible travel: for eco-
logical or fair trade aspects

(*) Telephone numbes that
are not toll-free

**PRICE CATEGORIES
HOTELS**

Expensive over 160 euros

Moderate 80–160 euros

Budget under 80 euros

Prices are for a double room
in peak season. Breakfast is
usually included

**PRICE CATEGORIES
RESTAURANTS**

Expensive over 30 euros

Moderate 15–30 euros

Budget under 15 euros

Prices are for starter, main
course and dessert including
table wine

CONTENTS

DID YOU KNOW?
Timeline → p. 14
Local specialities → p. 28
For bookworms & film buffs
→ p. 41
National holidays → p. 111
Budgeting → p. 117
Currency converter → p. 118
Weather → p. 119

MAPS IN THE GUIDEBOOK
(126 A1) Page numbers and
coordinates refer to the road
atlas
(O) Site/address located off
the map
Coordinates are also given for
places that are not marked
on the road map
(U A1) Coordinates refer to
the street maps of Maó and
Ciutadella inside the back
cover

(*A–B 2–3*) refers to the
removable pull-out map
(*a–b 2–3*) refers to the
additional map on the pull-
out map

INSIDE FRONT COVER:
The best Highlights

INSIDE BACK COVER:
Street maps of Maó and
Ciutadella

The best MARCO POLO Insider Tips

Our top 15 Insider Tips

INSIDER TIP **Tasty medicine**
Menorcan *chamomile flowers* are a well-known traditional panacea and – in case you're not a fan of Chamomile tea – is really tasty as chamomile liqueur → **p. 31**

INSIDER TIP **First class views of the port**
From the end of the short alleyway *Carrer d'Alfons III* you will find the best view of extensive Port de Maó and its many boats (photo right) → **p. 39**

INSIDER TIP **On the town walls**
From the *Bastió des Governador* in Ciutadella you can cast your gaze as far as the lighthouse at the mouth of the port → **p. 80**

INSIDER TIP **Underground nights**
"Singing, laughing, having a wonderful time" – that's how a regular sums up this bar. You'll find the best atmosphere on weekends at *Es Cau*, a cave bar in Es Castell → **p. 35**

INSIDER TIP **Hikes for those with steady nerves**
The adventurous hiking tours through the unspoilt *Barranc d'Algendar* are ideal for both hiking fans and nature lovers – experienced guides ensure that no one gets lost → **p. 104**

INSIDER TIP **Every Tuesday**
Hot summer evenings: On Tuesday nights, the historic district of Maó is where the party is. During the *Nits de Música al Carrer,* the shops stay open longer and there are special deals on tapas. Bands play to warm up the crowds → **p. 43**

INSIDER TIP **Gourmet in a quarry**
The light sandstone walls in the restaurant *Sa Pedrera d'es Pujol* are reminiscent of the old quarry that used to be here, but the meals created by Daniel and Nuria are as modern as it gets: the finest Menorcan cuisine → **p. 50**

INSIDER TIP High C in the cloister

Delightful sounds fill the otherwise quiet cloister of the old seminary in Ciutadella during the summer music festival, the *Festival de Música d'Estiu* → p. 110

INSIDER TIP Boating to a beautiful bay

Menorca's idyllic bay can be a bit tricky to get to, but it's easy to experience the *Cala Macarella* if you approach it from the water – and you'll also get to see the gorgeous southern coast in the process → p. 87

INSIDER TIP Paddling in the lagoon

The water in the almost entirely enclosed bay of *Fornells* is so still that even newbies are happy to climb into a kayak or onto a paddleboard. When the water is clear, you can see all the way to the bottom → p. 55

INSIDER TIP Relax in a historic villa

Peacocks in the garden and organic, home-grown produce for breakfast, the *Son Granot* finca is a fine place to relax and feel good → p. 35

INSIDER TIP Sundown relaxation

Sink into the soft cushions of the patio seats at beach club *Isabella* with a drink in your hand while the sun sets into the lagoon of Fornells → p. 55

INSIDER TIP Walking with a sheep

On the "Sunday of the Sheep" at the start of the *St John the Baptist* celebrations in June, a farmer's son carries a lamb on his shoulders through Ciutadella → p. 110

INSIDER TIP Sweet seduction

You can get *turrón* – the sweet almond and honey speciality typical of the Balearic Islands – in all its delicious varieties at the specialists *El Turronero* in the centre of Maó (photo left) → p. 42

INSIDER TIP Lodgings with charme

An old palace, lovingly restored and featuring trendy design: *Jardí de ses Bruixes* is Maó's most beautiful hotel. Enjoy your breakfast in art nouveau ambience! → p. 45

BEST OF...

FOR FREE

● *Green view from the tower*

The largest environmental organisation on the island *(GOB Menorca)* has its base in the capital at the *Molí del Rei* (the king's mill) which has splendid views of Maó town and harbour. Admission is free → p. 38

● *Archaische Architektur*

Want to explore Menorca's prehistoric era? You can visit one of the largest and most beautiful settlements for free, and it's thousands of years old: *Talaiot de Trepucó* → p. 46

● *Green and free*

You can visit the protected wetlands *S'Albufera d'es Grau* – with its rich variety of flora and fauna – on your own or as part of a group tour, and the best thing about it is that the guides are free (photo) → p. 56

● *Free open-air observatory*

Some places on the north coast are so free of light pollution that after sunset you can see thousands of stars with the naked eye. One of the best places not only for hobby astronomers is *Punta Nati* on the north-western tip of the island → p. 88

● *Free wireless internet connection*

Although you are usually charged for using WiFi on Menorca, the local government is now setting up free WiFi zones on all of the Balearic beaches – the project is called "IB-WiFi Playas" → p. 117

● *Parking is free at the beach*

Access and parking at most of the island's unspoilt beaches is once again free of charge. And you can save the 5 euros parking fee for *Calas Macarella* and *Macarelleta* by using the first car park (not far from the beach) and taking a short walk → p. 87

◖◗◖◗◗ Dots in guidebook refer to "Best of..." tips

On horseback

Horses are to Menorca what Edelweiss is to the Alps. Experience the beautiful creatures on a trail ride (photo) by booking with a company like *Cavalls Son Àngel* – or attend celebrations like *Festes de la Verge de Gràcia* in Maó → p. 109, 111

Agritourism

Enjoy a stylish and atmospheric stay in an old country house converted into a hotel, such as the *Binigaus Vell*: old Menorcan tools, rough plastered walls in gleaming white and modern 4-star comforts → p. 70

Lobster stew

Not cheap, but the original *caldereta* – preferably served in an earthenware *olla* – in a restaurant such as *La Guapa* in Fornells, is as much a part of a Menorca holiday as the missing corners of the island's cheese → p. 54

Sunken fortresses

The majority of fortresses were constructed in the era of piracy and colonial wars. Nature has reclaimed many of the buildings in the meantime, but some of them were preserved, such as the fortress *La Mola* and the *Castell de Sant Felip* near Maó → p. 46, 35

In search of everyday Menorcan cuisine

Erected in the middle of the 19th century and renovated during the 21st century, the *Mercat* (market) in Ciutadella, tiled in green and white, has a timeless quality. Here you can look over the shoulders of Menorcan women as they go about their shopping → p. 79

The cradle of civilisation

How did the indigenous people manage to erect these colossal structures? There are many prehistoric stone formations on Menorca, even if they are often in ruins today. One of the most impressive stone formations is the ruins of an entire city, *Torre d'en Galmés* → p. 65

Carribean flair

Typical of Menorca's sunny south side are the ravines which run out into small coves with fine, white sand against the backdrop of the turquoise sea. A good example is *Cala Trebalúger* near Cala Galdana → p. 69

BEST OF...

● **Jazz in the cellar vaults**
In the cosy *La Cava del Ars* in Maó they serve not only delicious tapas and tasty island wines, but from time to time there are also jazz sessions → p. 41

● **Fierce intensity**
Thundering cannons, a sea of flags, the heat of battle. Experience the historical siege of the island – in virtual form only, luckily! – at the massive *Fort Marlborough* near Es Castell → p. 107

● **Spain's oldest opera house**
Built in 1829, the treasured *Teatre* in Maó is so small that you can almost touch the artists on the stage. The music performed ranges from classic to jazz and even opera in November → p. 44

● **History and anecdotes**
Menorcan history, traditional crafts, paintings and engravings by Menorcan artists: the *Museu de Menorca* in Maó offers lots of diversions→ p. 38

● **Gift of God, not only for rainy days**
Gothic splendour in the Ciutadella *cathedral:* High columns, filigree windows, and expressive sculptures adorn the island's historic church (photo) → p. 78

● **A quieter spot for souvenir shopping**
From the beautiful to the bizarre: The *Centre Artesanal de Menorca* in Es Mercadel offers handicrafts of all kinds from local artisans. Watching them at work never gets boring, even if you're just popping in to wait out a long rain shower. And if a unique and special piece catches your eye, you can take it home with you directly → p. 108

RAIN

RELAX AND CHILL OUT
Take it easy and spoil yourself

● To "cock pigeon island"
Take a boat from the quayside at Es Grau to the tiny offshore island of *Illa d'en Colom,* which is home to marine birds and lizards. There are two wonderful beaches on the island where you can enjoy a picnic while gazing over to Menorca → **p. 58**

● Sundowner at the quayside
Round off your day in style with a glass of Menorcan wine at one of the *street bars* in Es Castell while watching the boats leave the harbour for the wide open seas → **p. 35**

● A day at the beach
The *Cales Coves* ("cave bays") offer an ideal spot for relaxation: Protected from the wind by the surrounding cliffs, the water in the bay is calm and crystal clear. Enjoy a fun day at the beach here (photo) → **p. 49**

● Jazz in a cave
A historic bar at the Ciutadella harbour: At Sa Clau, you can often enjoy live jazz alongside a perfectly mixed mojito or daiquiri. If it's too windy on the harbour-side terrace, you can always warm up in the rustic natural cave → **p. 84**

● Spanish Carribean
The 20-minute trek on foot to *Cala Mitjana* is well worth the effort: a fine sandy white beach with shallow, turquoise water awaits you. Hidden among pine trees in a rocky bay, it offers a delightful spot for bathing and a picnic → **p. 69**

● Easygoing beachside bar
At the Sant Adeodat beach in *Es Bruc* on Menorca's south coast you can enjoy reasonably-priced fresh seafood in a relaxed setting, topped off with splendid views out to sea → **p. 72**

CHILL OUT

INTRODUCTION

DISCOVER MENORCA!

On Menorca, you'll often hear the phrase *a poc a poc,* which, loosely translated, means something like "slowly, slowly..." The islanders like to take *time for the good things in life*, for friends and family, good food and drink, enjoying nature and simply daydreaming. Driving, ordering in a restaurant, shopping – everything is done at a leisurely pace. Could it be the breath-taking local landscapes that make the islanders so relaxed? Everywhere you look, you'll see *stunning bays with clear, turquoise water* below a gorgeous blue sky, pale stone in shades ranging from beige to red, fragrant pine forests and hilly pastures.

The Menorcans have also created small oases of relaxation within the cities: Even the bleakest of streets is perked up by a bistro bar with the typical folding chairs on the pavement. People meet there for a quick *pomada (gin with lemonade)* and to share the news of the day. The Menorcan lifestyle also includes a *refreshing dip in the sea* – best repeated daily, but the weekends are a must, at bare minimum. And you won't need to travel far to swim, as there's a beautiful bay waiting right around every corner.

Ambient location: Fortalesa Isabel II on the peninsula of La Mola at the entrance to the harbour of Maó

That's why Menorca is rightly considered the *sweeter, quieter* of the Balearic Islands when compared to its rowdier sisters, even during the high season. It's farther from the Spanish mainland and was developed later than Mallorca and Ibiza, which helped it avoid many of the side effects of mass tourism – you won't find enormous concrete hotels or throngs of drunken, bellowing tourists here. Visitors to Menorca love the idyllic bays, romantic historic districts and mysterious relics from the distant past.

Fiords, mythical creatures, cornfields and beaches

Although the island is relatively small, it has *two very diferent sides*. Tramuntana in the north is characterised by *calas,* deep fjords which have carved their way into the interior, bizarre rock formations and an irregular coastline with a series of natural harbours. Here the landscape is dominated by dark rocks which, shaped by wind and sea, give many parts of the coastline a *rugged character* and the area has always been more scarcely populated than the centre and the south coast. The north belonged to mythical creatures and gods. There are numerous island legends attached

ca. 2800 BC
First settlers from southern France and the Iberian Peninsula

1500 BC
Talaiot culture: Construction of large cult buildings and walled towns

205 BC
Hannibal's brother, General Magon, arrives on Menorca and establishes Maó

From 123 BC
Roman occupation and decline of the *talaiot* culture

903–1287
Arab occupation; Menorca is annexed to the Caliphate of Córdoba

to sites along the windswept north coast while in the north-western parts of the island one encounters large areas of pasture land. Golden cornfields and flowers transform the landscape in spring and autumn into a *spectacular blaze of colour*. The vegetation often extends right down to the coast, clinging ever more tightly to the rocky soil. Only the outermost tips of land, the capes, are completely barren. Here, on stormy days in the autumn or spring, the sea spray showers the dark coastal cliffs with a white deposit of salt.

The Migjorn in the south is completely different, with a more sheltered coastline made up of small bays, wooded valleys and gorges. The southern part of Menorca consists of a 50–60 m/160–200 ft high limestone plateau which gently slopes to the south and is only interrupted by the course of drainage channels. This is where *Menorca's sunny side shows itself*, with a lighter, more Mediterranean architecture and pine trees rising up into the sky, largely sheltered from the strong winds from the Gulf of Lion which, on more than a hundred days in the year, mainly during the winter, sweep across the north of the island at speeds of more than 100 km/60 mph. Most of the beaches are situated in the south, which is why most tourists are drawn there.

Oases of relaxation and a refreshing dip in the sea

If you take a look at the map, you'll immediately spot Menorca's exposed location. It looks like a boomerang tossed into the sea 45 km/28 miles off the coast of Mallorca – almost equidistant from Africa and the Spanish mainland. Visitors can look forward to *warm, sunny weather:* average temperatures of more than 25 degrees in the summer and 14 degrees in winter, with more than 2,450 hours of sunshine per

1287
In the course of the Reconquista Menorca is recovered by Alfonso III of Aragon

After 1500
Pirates attack and destroy Maó (1535) and Ciutadella (1558)

1712
Great Britain takes possession of Menorca

1782
Duke Crillon captures the island from the British on behalf of the Spanish crown

1798
The British land on Menorca for the third time and British defence towers are built on the coast

year. In the troika comprising Mallorca, Menorca and Ibiza, Menorca is solidly in the middle of the Balearic Islands, with a size of 700 km²/270 sq miles. Just *90,000 people live on the island* – but only during the high season in summer. In October, many of the island's regular residents leave along with the visitors, preferring to spend the winter with relatives on the Spanish mainland.

The two sides of the island are also as different as the north and south coast. In the east is the British-influenced, hard-working *Maó*, and in the west the more rebellious and permissive Spanish *Ciutadella*. The differences are not only in the architecture, but also in the outlook on life. Competition between the cities began with the British occupation. In the early 18th century, the British relocated the capital city from Ciutadella to Maó, because Maó had a better natural harbour. For Ciutadella, this meant that the local nobility and clergy were cut off from the important decision-making processes they had formerly controlled. Maó's citizens, on the other hand, benefitted from English rule. That's why even today, true Ciutadella natives prefer to avoid going to Maó. They only go if they have errands to take care of or unavoidable appointments at government offices to keep.

> **Guard towers, tables, ships: enormous, ancient stone structures**

Menorca's historical roots go deep into the past. People are believed to have inhabited the island more than 6500 years ago, the *first settlers* settlers probably having come across the sea on reed boats. Some rock wall drawings in the caves of Menorca depict boats which bear a strong resemblance to similar illustrations on Crete. The oldest remains – imperishable stone buildings assembled without mortar – are up to *4000 years old*. Some of them are still awaiting interpretation, especially the prehistoric caves and settlements with their stone tables *(taules)* and towers *(talaiots)*, as well as the chamber tombs *(navetas)* which are shrouded in legend and probably the *oldest preserved buildings in Europe*. Later Phoenicians, Greeks, Carthaginians and Romans used the island's strategic location while the Byzantines and finally the Arabs subjugated it.

It was not until 1287, as the final act of the *Christian reconquest* of Spain as it were, that Menorca was once more wrested from the hands of the "infidels" – which, for

1802
The Treaty of Amiens places Menorca under Spanish rule

1936–39
Menorca, a bastion of the Republicans in the Spanish Civil War, falls to the forces of General Franco's troops

1953
The first tourist charter plane lands on the island

1983
The Balearics become a Comunitat Autónoma, also establishing the right to their own language

1993
Unesco declares the island of Menorca a Biosphere Reserve

Menorca's splendid beaches and bays are the island's hallmark, such as Cala Mitjana

the inhabitants of the island at that time, was not necessarily a turn for the better. Famine and epidemics were the consequence and it was only the occupation of Menorca by the British which re-established trade, craft and culture. Today around 60 per cent of all the islanders are directly or indirectly involved in tourism. And yet there is a determination to place more emphasis on *environmental-conscious individual holidaymakers* rather than on mass tourism. It seems that Menorca is consciously seeking to avoid making the mistakes of its big and little sisters to the

> **Relaxing holiday in unspoiled nature**

south-west. It understands the *Reserva de la Biosfera* designation not just as a clever marketing ploy, and very much wants to prove that a reasonable amount of tourism can be perfectly suited to intact social and cultural structures and a *largely unspoilt natural landscape*. In keeping with the motto: *Ets Menorca, no frissis!* – You're on Menorca, so take your time and don't rush! Adapt to the rhythm of the island and let your five senses be your guide. You won't regret it!

2005
Menorca is the first of the Balearic islands to commit itself to "Local Agenda 21", the programme for sustainable development

2015
Environmental activists and the Balearic government successfully campaign against boring for crude oil in the west of the Mediterranean

2017
The construction of new hotels is approved to handle the onslaught of tourists

WHAT'S HOT

1 Catch of the day

From the market to your mouth The *Mercat des Peix*, the
Maó fish market (photo), sells the catch of the day, which
is also served up to the patrons in the area's chic seafood
restaurants. In that sense, it stands to reason that you'll
only find the very freshest fish on your plate here! The fish
market in Ciutadella is even more relaxed: You can
take the fish you've just bought to *Ulises* next
door and have them fry it up for you. It's busi-
est on Saturday nights!

Bye, grapevine louse! 2

The world of winegrowing The phylloxera grape-
vine louse destroyed nearly all the vineyards in Menorca. They've only recently begun to experience a
revival, and the best part? They're open to visitors.
*Bodega Binifadet (Cami De Ses Barraques | www.
binifadet.com) (photo)* in Sant Lluis paved the way.
Merluzo – "hake" – is the name of its light, fruity
wine that pairs perfectly with fresh seafood. After a
wine tasting with commentary, you can take a tour of
the winery and vineyard. *Bodega Binitord (www.binitord.
com)* is also open to visitors: Its exquisite wines are produced just south of Ciutadella, in a former quarry.

3 Menorca Challenge

Hike, Bike, Swim Growing numbers of Menorcans want to experience the island in a more active way. They burn off
their energy in sporting competitions – and natural-
ly, visitors to the island participate, as well. The
Trail dels Fars, a 44-km/27 mile run in Febru-
ary, starts at the lighthouse *(far)* on the *Cap
de Cavalleria.* The *Half Menorca (artiemhalf
menorca.com)* is scheduled for September;
this event really packs a punch. It's a triath-
lon: 1.9 km/1.2mile swimming, 21 km/13

miles running, 90 km/56 miles cycling. There's also a streamlined version for people who want to take it a bit easier. The season concludes in mid-October with the *Vuelta a Menorca (menorcacicloturista.com):* cycling around the entire island.

Flavourful herbs

4

Gin with Menorcan plants Since the era of British occupation, gin *(photo)* has been the national beverage of Menorca. A young generation of distillers is now experimenting with new, typically Menorcan flavours. At the *Finca L'Enzell (innatgin.com)* at the foot of Monte Toro, they produce premium gin under the brand name iNNat. The tangy drink is distilled with pine branches, thyme, lemon and forest fruits. The new Gin Glop Menorca *(ginglop.com)* also tastes fresh and fruity; the island herbs that give it its flavour are displayed on the black bottle.

Island lifestyle

5

Local products *Avarques,* the Menorcan sandals with a flat rubber sole, heel strap, and "toe holder", have always been a bestseller. Now, Joan Doblas has come up with a humorous version of the shoe, with a sole in the shape of Menorca, that he sells in his shop *Ca'n Doblas (Plaça Jaume II | Ferreries |www.candoblas. com) (photo)*. Jewellery designers find inspiration in the island's labyrinthine quarries: *Lithica,* "stone age", *(www.lithica.es)* is the name of the collection with the archaic labyrinth logo. And if you want to feel the island melt in your mouth, pay a visit to the delicatessen *El Paladar (C/ Ciutadella 97 | Maó | www.elpaladar.es)* – it only carries treats produced on the island.

19

IN A NUTSHELL

BIRDWATCHING

Don't forget your earplugs when you hike to Punta S'Escullar! The chirping, twittering and screeching that you'll often encounter here is so deafening that it even drowns out the sound of the fierce waves crashing on the northern coastline. Flocks of Scopoli's shearwaters flutter overhead – marine birds related to the albatross. A whopping 1 million couples – couples! – live in the desolate cliffs located a 30-minute walk west of Cala Morell. It's the largest colony in this part of the Mediterranean. Incidentally, Scopoli's shearwaters don't like to be approached, and they will take revenge by emptying their bowels on the nearest target...

The fact that birds feel so comfortable on Menorca is down to the island's location between Europe and Africa. In fact, some of these feathered creatures enjoy Menorca so much that they never want to leave – including the kingfisher, which is easily identified by its bright blue and orange feathers, as well as the black-and-white-striped and "mohawked" Eurasian hoopoe and the white-headed red kite. If you see a white body with dark-edged wings flying high above you, it's probably a black vulture (*alimoche* in Spanish), which has also settled here and even become Menorca's mascot. The best areas for birdwatching are the S'Albufera des Grau marshes on the east coast and Prat de Son Bou on the southern coast – you can join guided bird-

Photo: Estate near Ferreries

Tanques, taules, talaiots: a cross section of Menorca's idiosyncrasies, history and nature

watching tours there *(menorcawalking birds.com)*.

BINI WHAT?

Pretty soon, your head will be swimming from all the place names that start with "Bini": Binibèquer, Binifancolla, Biniarocca, Binillautí... Where on earth does this prefix come from? But to Arabic speakers, the origin of the term is immediately clear: Bini means "property of the sons of..." and implies that the places once belonged to the sons of

Bèquer, Fancolla, Rocca and Llautí. The Arabic prefix "Al" also appears frequently, in names such as "Alaior". These geographical descriptions are the legacy of the Arabs, who conquered the Balearic Islands in 903 A.D. after taking the Iberian mainland. They were quite tolerant towards those of other faiths – Christians and Jews were allowed to practise their religion without restriction. The Christian conquerors, on the other hand, spoke a very different language: one of violence and military might. When King Alfonso III of Aragon captured the Balearic Islands in 1287, the Arabs were enslaved, their property looted, their mosques razed. In fact, the Ciutadella cathedral was once

Not a single concrete hotel block as far as the eye can see – like here at Cala Galdana

an enormous Muslim house of worship – but it's barely recognisable as such today.

COOL

"Better in winter": This is the slogan Menorca is using to attract new visitors. And it's the truth! It might be somewhat inconvenient to get to Menorca from Barcelona in the cooler months (October to mid-May), but the off-peak season offers a number of advantages. The meadows burst into bloom with the first autumn rains, creating alpine pastures where cows suddenly emerge from their shady summer stalls to graze. The Menorcans refer to this phenomenon as "our au-

tumn-spring". The restaurants that are still open during this season are mainly frequented by locals; traditional holidays are celebrated, and the locals hold sporting events for which the summer weather would be far too hot. Incidentally, the off-peak season is also much nicer for hiking or cycling. The one problem is that many hotels in popular holiday destinations are closed, so it's better to book in Ciutadella or Maó.

WHITE, WHITER, WHITEST

Why are the buildings painted with so much white paint when the sun is just going to bleach the stone anyway? It turns out that there are environmental reasons for the thick coating: Wind and rain tends to destroy the facades of buildings made of sand-lime brick *(marés)*, particularly in the north of the island, so the islanders protect their homes with a thick layer of lime that they apply once a year. This practice has been in place for as long as anyone can remember. Today, many people use modern emulsion paint, even on the roofs and the clay rain gutters that direct rainwater into underground cisterns. The homesteads look particularly impressive painted brilliant white and perched on a hilltop – little castles whose owners look down on their estates like kings.

NO BEACHES WITHOUT RAIN

It's not exactly massive: The largest mountain on Menorca is just 357 m/1,170 ft high. Based on that, you wouldn't expect the island to have particularly diverse landscapes. But it does, thanks to the *barrancs* – barrancos in Spanish – gullies created by running water, cut into the soft limestone by millennia of rain. There are 36 of them in the south of the island; they stretch on for kilometres toward the coast and create fantastic beaches on their delta. The confluence of two *barrancs* in Son Bou is particularly beautiful; dunes and wetlands have formed in the area. The *Barranc de Binigaus* is also stunning – a deep green thicket with enormous caves. And in the *Barranc d'Algendar,* which winds from Ferreries to Cala Galdana, a forest of pines and cork oaks has formed, making it a perfect place for hiking. The fact that the *barrancs* are usually lush and green is due to more than just the water that collects during rainfall; the canyon walls, which reach heights of up to 40 m/131 ft, also protect the gullies from the cold Tramuntana wind, creating a mild microclimate. The first settlers came to live in the southern *barrancs* – they knew where the living was good!

FAREWELL, ARCHITECTURAL EYESORES

Since the 1960s, the neighbouring island of Mallorca has been paving over one stretch of coastline after the next. The founding of a "Group to Protect Birds and Nature" *(www.gobmenorca.com)* in 1971 was a first humble attempt at stopping the destruction of the Balearic Islands. It wasn't until 20 years later that a nature conservation law went into effect – and it was fiercely enforced on Menorca. A whopping 43 per cent of the island's land was protected by the nature conservation law (the European average is just 7 per cent!), and building on the coast is prohibited, with the exception of the territory of Ciutadella and south of Maó. The northern half of Menorca (Tramuntana) is also closed to construction projects, as are large swaths of the island's inland regions. And in 1993, conservation efforts were augmented once again: Menorca was named a UNESCO

Biosphere Reserve *(www.biosferamenorca.org)*. It might sound like a marketing tactic, a sort of meaningless banner that the Menorcans proudly display to attract tourists, but no – it's a process, and every year, they have to prove that they aren't sacrificing environmental protection on the altar of economic development. In order to lend weight to these claims, Menorca's municipalities have also committed to upholding the UN Agenda Local 21, which states that the economy is geared toward sustainable development so that future generations will continue to be able to enjoy Menorca's nature.

REALLY LESI

Menorca is the island of the British. And it's no wonder: Great Britain ruled Menorca for 71 years. The British occupied the island three times, in increasingly shorter time spans: first from 1706 to 1754, then from 1763 to 1782, then finally from 1798 to 1802, before they ultimately returned the island to Spain for good. And what remains of that colonial heritage? The black-and-white checked "Friesian" cows that the British brought along to produce large quantities of high-fat milk to make good cheese are the most obvious remnant, but British gin is also ubiquitous – it's essentially Menorca's national drink. Sailors and soldiers taught the Menorcans how to distil it from purified alcohol and juniper. And you will run into many English words that have been so corrupted over time that it's nearly impossible to recognise them: For example, you can close the *vindou* (window), eat *bifi* (beef) for lunch, or have a quick drink – *ha fet un trinqui* (from to drink), which will make you feel *lesi* (lazy). The massive *Fort Marlborough* near Maó, with its cannons and casemates, is also part of the British legacy. Nearby is Georgetown (today known as Es Castell), a garrison city with a military training ground, barracks, and roads arranged in a grid. The British are additionally responsible for the first (!) road connecting east and west, which they constructed in 1722 and which is still named after Governor Richard Kane (*Camí d'en Kane*) today. Incidentally, Kane wasn't viewed as an evil occupier by any means, but rather as a liberator from a backward feudal system. And the British primarily valued Menorca as an important base of military operations in the Mediterranean, a stepping stone between Gibraltar – which they already controlled at that point – and the Middle East, which they had set their sights on.

B EG PARDON?

The islanders generally understand Spanish, but they aren't too keen on speaking it. So you may find that if you ask a question in Spanish, you'll receive an answer in *Menorquí,* and then you'll probably understand *nada* – nothing at all. If this happens, you might find English a bit more helpful. In any case, Menorcans are proud that they "speak differently than the people from Madrid", and they want to emphasise that they also think and act differently than their distant Castilian cousins: They see themselves as more relaxed, friendlier, less dominant. *Menorquí,* the Menorcan dialect, is one of the oldest dialects of *Català,* or Catalan, still in use today; Catalan was brought over from Aragon by King Alfonso III in 1287. *Català* has been recognised since 1983 as an official language on the Balearics with equal status to Castilian Spanish and now enjoys great popularity amongst the younger generation after the years of suppression of all regional languages under the Franco dictatorship. Place names on road signs are now almost only in the Catalan variant. *Català* is

spoken in schools and at the University of the Balearic Islands, books are written in or translated into Catalan. And as many Catalonians would like to break away from Spain, it's likely that the Spanish language will continue to be pushed farther into the background as time goes on.

M AYO FROM MAÓ

Mayonnaise in your salad isn't a completely unfamiliar sight. But where does this famous dip come from originally? The proof that this white sauce originated on Menorca isn't yet 100% definitive, but there are many signs that point to the French Duke of Richelieu. During the brief period that France ruled the island (seven years in the mid-18th century), it's said that Richelieu helped mayonnaise achieve global fame. The Frenchman did more than just steal the heart of a woman from Maó (Spanish: *mahonesa); he* also learned a few secrets of Menorcan cuisine from her, including a simple, rustic recipe that farmers used to eat to replenish their strength after a long, hard day in the fields: olive oil mixed with egg, a pinch of salt, and crushed garlic. It's very possible that this Balearic *alli oli* (garlic with oil) became its elegant, garlic-free French cousin, and that the *mahonesa's* sauce became mayonnaise.

P REHISTORIC STRUCTURES

Relics of a prehistoric age might not sound terribly exciting. Prehistoric ritual sites...a bit more interesting! Stone tables where human sacrifices were performed? Now that's gruesome! "Talaiot" (2500–123 B.C.) is the name used to describe the society that existed on Menorca during the Iron Age which erected impressive megaliths. Although these monuments can be found on the other Balearic islands, Menorca has the most with a total of 1600 sites, 274 of which are well-maintained remains. They are spread across the island with the most found in the island's fertile south. The word *talaiot* originates from the Arabic word *atalaya* (lookout tower) and indeed most of the monuments are situated on mounts. There are three types of constructions: *talaiots* ("lookout towers"), *taules* ("tables") and *navetas* ("ships") shaped like a ship's hull facing keel-side up. It is presumed that these were used as graves. *Talaiots* are round or rectangular-shaped structures made of large stones without the use of mortar. The *taules* can be up to 3 m in height and consist of vertical pillars with a horizontal stone lying on them. Although their exact meaning is unknown, one theory is they were the place where Celtic Druids performed human sacrifices. It is more likely, however, that the *taules* themselves represented a deity, for example a bull. The central stone T is almost always surrounded by a circle of monoliths. The whole complex, where a fire constantly burned and animal sacrifices were made, was almost certainly used for ritual purposes.

STONE BY STONE

A wall nearly as long as the Great Wall of China? You can find it on the little island of Menorca! If you look out the window as your plane is landing, it will look like an enormous puzzle at first. And once you're on the island, you'll realise what it's all about: The puzzle pieces are fields *(tanques)* separated from one another by walls *(parets)* 1 to 1.50 m/3 to 5 ft high. For centuries, the farmers of Menorca took upon themselves the Sisyphean task of piling these cobblestones together without mortar. If you add all the walls of Menorca together, they come out to the enormous length of 20,000 km/12,425 miles, just 1,000 km/620 miles shorter than the Great Wall of China. And what are the walls for? Simple: The farmers wanted to get the stones off the fields to make them easier to cultivate, and the walls protected plants from the wind and created enclosures for their precious livestock.

What are they picking there? Crocuses? No, it's saffron, well-protected by a stone wall

FOOD & DRINK

Bon profit! **Even if the prices of some** *caldereta* **suggest the opposite – this enthusiastic greeting is not uttered for the landlord's benefit, rubbing his hands eagerly as he presents you with the bill, but is simply expressing the wish that you will enjoy your meal.**

On Menorca there are some *540 restaurants* (with seating for more than 30,000) as well as a good 660 bars and cafés. The Balearic authorities provide a rather superficial quality classification – referring mainly to cleanliness, furnishing and seating capacity – for restaurants (forks as a symbol), bars (goblets) and cafeterias (cups). One symbol indicates a basic standard and three the very best quality. Just under a third of the premises on Menorca are *pure holiday businesses*, closing down when the season comes to an end, and they generally provide more or less good "international" cuisine, i.e. steak, chicken, hamburgers and occasionally fish, usually with a generous portion of chips and some salad. Once you've tried it, you know pretty well how it is going to taste everywhere else, and you may then be more curious to find out what else is simmering in the island's *greixoneres* and *olles* (clay pots and bowls). It is worth being a bit adventurous, you will not be disappointed. *Menorca's cuisine is simple, rich, hearty* and very tasty. Cultures which were historically incompatible come together in the saucepan, simple Arab and Catalan recipes, for example, are given a British touch or enhanced by

The table spread is produce from the sea and fields: simple, honest, rooted in nature – Menorca's authentic cuisine is back in favour

a subtle soupçon of French flair. **Everything that is served comes from the sea and the fields**, including typical vegetables such as tomatoes, artichokes, peas, beans, onions, potatoes, carrots and cabbage. And there is game, lamb, veal, pork and lots of fresh fish and other seafood – all preferably prepared with garlic, olive oil and the island's aromatic herbs such as rosemary and thyme.

Caldereta is now a very upmarket meal. It is **red lobster cooked in a delicate ve-**

getable broth (the basic recipe is: onion, two cloves of garlic, tomato, leek, seasoned with two tablespoons of brandy and a sprig of parsley). A portion costs about 80 euros, but for this rather steep price you are invited to select your own live lobster, which is then transformed into culinary delicacy in the saucepan.

As soon as you arrive at the airport you will encounter piles of *ensaïmadas*, a delicious, light, spiral-shaped **pastry**. It comes in various sizes and with different fillings, such as *cabello de ángel* (pump-

LOCAL SPECIALITIES

Albergínies al forn – baked aubergines, the aubergine halves are filled with a bread, egg, spices and aubergine flesh mixture and baked in the oven; variation: baked courgette *(carabassons al forn)*

Arròs brut – "dirty rice": rice dish with meat, black pudding, peas, beans, garlic and herbs

Calamar farcit – stuffed squid: gently fried squid that is stuffed with a mixture of coarse bread crumbs, parsley, garlic, egg and pine nuts and then braised in the oven (photo right)

Caragols – snails (done the Menorcan way) that are fed for three days on flour, then cooked in a herb stock (made up of bay leaves, garlic, parsley, onions and tomato) and served with aioli

Coca de verdura – yeast dough pizza topped with vegetables

Conill amb cebes – rabbit with onions is usually cooked in a *greixonera*, a typical clay pot. Other varieties alsocombine rabbit with lobster and other seafood

Greixonera de brossat – curd cheese baked in a flat clay pot with lemon zest and cinnamon, a light creamy dessert

Llom amb col – a pork and cabbage stew cooked with white wine, bacon, tomatoes, onions, garlic and thyme in a clay pot

Oli i aigua – a tomato and vegetable soup, served in clay bowls and with thin slices of bread

Olla de mongetes – substantial bean soup with onions, tomatoes, garlic and white beans

Peix en es forn – halibut, redfish or a similar fish is baked in the oven with potatoes, raisins, pine nuts, spinach and tomatoes

Perdiu amb col – guinea fowl breasts are gently fried and then cooked in a clay pot. Cabbage leaves dusted with flour are fried in oil until golden and then served in the clay pot with the guinea fowl

Pilotes – tiny meatballs in a tomato or almond sauce, available in most bars as tapas (photo left)

Pomada/Gin amb Limonada – Gin with lemonade

Sofrit – vegetable dish made of onions, peppers, tomatoes and garlic, as a side dish or as a topping for flat bread *(coques)*

kin jam), *crema* (crème patissière) and *nata* (whipped cream), and is to be found in almost all the bakeries on the island. The most important aspect in making it is that pork lard is used (which gives it its name, as *saïm* means lard). However, *crespells*, though equally sweet and sprinkled with icing sugar, are dry and crumble easily. Just like the *rubiolls*, they are made from a firm biscuit dough which is rolled out and can be filled with pumpkin jam or a sweet crème patissière. And finally there are also the *bunyols,* mainly available in the autumn, which are whorls (similar to small, hand-made doughnuts) made from a semi-liquid dough of flour or potato flour fried in hot oil. *Empanadas,* turnovers filled with vegetables, pork, lamb or a meat-vegetable mix, are *hearty and tasty*.

The best of the island's *cold meat products* is the *sobrasada*, a cured pork sausage which acquires its characteristic red colour from red bell peppers. It is often sliced and fried and even combined with honey or *ensaïmadas*. *Butifarrones* (black pudding) and *carn i xulla* (comparable to a coarse pepper salami) are also available everywhere, as is *Queso Maó-Menorca*, the famous *Menorcan cheese*. It has even been awarded the coveted guarantee of origin DOC (denominación de origen).

Just as there is no doubt that the British brought *gin* to Menorca, it is just as certain that that the people of Menorca have acquired a taste for the spirit. A distillery in Port de Maó produces it in the traditional way and there is another distillery which, since 2011, has been offering a Mediterranean variety under the brand name "Gin Mare". A popular and refreshing *island cocktail* is *pellofa*, gin with a generous splash of soda water and a slice of lemon. Copious amounts of *pomada*, a mix of gin and lemonade, are consumed, especially on feast days. *Herbes* (Spanish *hierbas*) comes originally from the Balearic island of Ibiza, further to the west, but Menorca also has some outstanding examples of this sweet, yellow herbal liqueur. The two regional specialities are the typical *Menorcan chamomile liqueur* as well as *palo*, a liqueur made from the fruits of the carob tree.

Need a quick pick-me-up? It looks like water, but it's gin

SHOPPING

Written off as a lost cause, Balearic arts and crafts have in recent years recovered significantly. A good example is Menorca. New, creative spirits are revisiting classic forms, traditional styles and old methods of production. The result is quite impressive: elegant leather shoes or, rather alternative, handmade *avarques* (sandals), leather bags, coats, jackets and trousers for every taste and purse.

You can also buy ceramics and ever more frequently artistic woodwork and traditional musical instruments too. The folding chairs covered with linen are also popular, and you can have them made in your favourite colour at *Sillas Menorca (Polígon Industrial de Ferreries | Ferreries | C/ Teulers 16 | www.sillasmenorca.com)*. In all the major resorts you will find *bisutería*, i.e. costume jewellery and paste gems. Fashionable accessories have been produced on the island since the 17th century.

ARTS AND CRAFTS

In July and August special arts and crafts markets are held every Wednesday evening (7–11pm) in Alaior and Thursday evening (7–10pm) in Es Mercadal.

CERAMICS

The individual pieces, or in fact the whole dinner service, are almost always hand painted. The predominant patterns are colourful rustic motifs, occasionally also simple British decoration. The pottery is made according to strict, traditional rules and there are only a few young potters who are nowadays prepared to make creative concessions.

CHAMOMILE

Essential oils, resins and glycosides give the dried flower heads of true chamomile or field chamomile (Catalan: *camamilla,* Spanish: *manzanilla)* a medicinal effect. It's more aromatic and a bit bitterer than the central European version; it is often used for infusions and distilled into liqueur. You can find real Menorca chamomile and chamomile liqueur at places like *Autèntic* (see p. 42) or *Sa Botiga d'es Centre (C/ Josep Maria Quadrado 8)* in Ciutadella.

CHEESE

It has hardly any aroma, has a semi-firm rind and, because of its square shape, it

The many family businesses and cottage enterprises have developed a remarkable penchant for the classic and elegant

is easy to store and transport: *Queso Maó-Menorca* (as it is been officially called since 1995). It is marketed under the brand names *Coinga, Sant Patrici* and *La Payesa* amongst others. Menorcan cheese is an ideal holiday gift which you can buy in most grocery stores or from a producer in Alaior. But beware: only about 30 per cent of the cheese is really homemade. The real article can be distinguished from its industrially produced cousins by the cotton cloth pattern (particularly visible at the corners) as well as by its spicier taste.

GIN, PALO, HERBES

Popular souvenirs are local gin – which the British brought to the island – and the dark brown, high-proof speciality *palo*, a liqueur made from melted sugar or carob tree fruit. *Hierbas* or *herbes,* the liqueur containing up to 40 different island herbs, actually comes from Ibiza, but you will find it in every bar on Menorca – which also applies to **INSIDER TIP** chamomile liqueur.

LEATHER

You can find leather goods made on the island in *Maó* at *Pons Quintana (C/ S'Arravaleta 21;* shoes), in *Alaior* at *Gomila (C/ Miguel de Cervantes 46;* shoes) in *Ciutadella* in the leather factory *Patricia (C/ Santandria)* and in their shop in the old town *(C/ des Seminari 40 | www.patricia.es)*. Mascaro produces fashionable, high quality leather accessories; they have shops at the airport, in *Ferreries (Polígono Industrial)* and in *Maó (C/ Ses Moreres 29 | www. jaimemascaro.es)*.

31

MAÓ/
EASTERN TIP

The charming and – by Menorcan standards – large city of Maó presents a contrast to the solitude of the rugged northern coast, the tranquillity of the biosphere reserve, the wetlands of Es Grau, and the narrow strip of sleepy hamlets and holiday resorts that line the southern coast.

You will definitely encounter the competition between Maó and Ciutadella during your visit; their rivalry has a long history. The contention between the east and the west of Menorca, between the cities of Ciutadella and Maó, has been smouldering for centuries. For many years, Ciutadella was the most important port and, consequently, the leading city on the island. That all changed with the arrival of the English, who occupied the island and made Maó the capital in 1722. Resistance against the dominance of "British Maó" was primarily concentrated among affluent families, who traditionally lived in Ciutadella.

Mao was different – welcoming the British almost as liberators, opening up new trading opportunities. So Richard Kane wasted no time and make Maó the island capital – especially since the city had a better natural harbour.

ES CASTELL

(131 E–F4) (*M J–K6*) **As you make your way along the mile-long "fjord" which ends in Maó, you will already see the impact British colonial thinking has had**

Merry Minorca: Maó has the British to thank for its status as the island's administrative and commercial centre

on the architecture of Es Castell: a rectangular town plan and a central main square surrounded by garrison buildings.

The former crown settlement of Georgetown, later renamed Villacarlos, and now called Es Castell (population 7900) has blossomed into a self-confident community. The highlight of this small town is the tranquil harbour *Cales Fonts*. Colourful boats bob at anchor, surrounded by charming bars and restaurants that are always packed. Some of the

Maó nightlife can also be found in the harbour area.

ANA LUISA

At "Ana Luisa" aka Francisco you'll know you're sitting at the seaside: Enjoy their paella loaded with prawns and calamari. Vegetarians will also find a wide selection of delicious dishes. *Closed Wed | C/ Moll d'en Pons (just below Hotel Hamilton) | tel. 6 49 08 36 75 | Moderate*

ES CASTELL

CAPRICHOSA

Trendy pizzeria with a sea view, also serves an affordable set menu. *C/ Cales Fonts 44 | tel. 9 71 36 61 58 | Moderate*

DINKUM BAR-RESTAURANTE

Ideal for fans of fresh fish. Located in the rocks on the waterfront, overlooking the port and in the evenings there is a roman-

The terrace has a stunning, panoramic view of the bay. There is a good and very reasonable lunch menu. *C/ de Sa Font 1 | tel. 9 71 35 47 88 | Moderate*

SHOPPING

There is a small artisan market on the port steps at *Cales Fonts* from June to

Bars, shops and restaurants line the port at Es Castell

tic candlelit atmosphere. *C/ Cales Fonts 20 | tel. 9 71 36 70 17 | Moderate–Expensive*

EL CHIVITO

The ideal place for a light snack: very good value for money, tasty meals and friendly staff. They serve delicious *bocadillos*. Popular with young clientele. *C/ Cales Fonts 25 | tel. 9 71 35 29 44 | Budget*

IRENE

You really get something for your money in this pretty restaurant: international cuisine with fresh, first class ingredients.

September *(daily 8pm–2am)*. The *Mercat Artesanal (Mon 7pm–midnight | C/ Miranda des Cales Fonts)* offers exclusive arts & crafts.

SPORTS & ACTIVITIES

You can book a taxi boat to take a private tour around the harbour or to ferry you across to Maó, the La Mola fortress or the island of Illa del Rei: *Water Taxi (May–Oct | tel. 6 16 42 88 91 | minimum of 2 persons, tickets are sold on board)*. Want to take the helm yourself? Learn how to sail at the *Club Náutico Es Castell (Miranda de Cales Fonts | tel. 9 71 36 58 84).*

ENTERTAINMENT

Sedate rather than lively: ● Along the pedestrian promenades Moll des Pons and Cales Fonts, small bars built into the rocks with terraces by the sea and a view of the harbour mouth create a pleasant atmosphere for a quiet, sociable evening. The relaxed *Chèspir (C/ Cales Fonts 47)* regularly offers live jazz – and if you don't like cocktails, you can always order a smoothie! The cave bar INSIDER TIP *Es Cau (daily from 10pm | C/ Cala Corb 5)* is cult among the Meorcans; for decades they have been playing island folk here.

WHERE TO STAY

EL ALMIRANTE

British charm, a fantastic location, and lots of history: The red villa above the bay of Maó was constructed on the orders of Admiral Collingwood in the 18th century, and the paintings, furniture and ambience are reminiscent of that era. But the rooms are modern; there's a large pool and tennis court in the garden. *39 rooms | Ctra. Maó-Es Castell | tel. 9 71 36 27 00 | www.hoteldelalmirante.com | Moderate*

INSIDER TIP SON GRANOT ☺
This feudal villa built in 1712 for the former chief engineer of the British Empire stands just 500 m/1640 ft away from the harbour. Set in extensive garden grounds with a splendid pool, you can enjoy the surroundings while eating breakfast on the terrace - most of the fresh produce is grown on the finca including organic vegetables, fruit and eggs. You can watch peacocks strutting around the grounds and may even spot a stray hen on the hotel's terrace. The rooms have roman-

tic four-poster queen size beds with balconies which offer amazing views. The villa has a fireplace room with extensive library and riding stables. You can also hire bikes to explore the island. Señora Carolina belongs to the villa and is always on hand with ideas of what to do in the area. *11 rooms | Ctra. de Sant Felip | tel. 9 71 35 55 55 | www.songranot.com | Moderate–Expensive*

INFORMATION

Ateneu Municipal de Es Castell | C/ Miranda de Cala Corb 10 | tel. 9 71 35 23 66 | turisme@aj-escastell.org

WHERE TO GO

CASTELL DE SANT FELIP ●
(131 E–F4) (*𝄢 K6*)
The road to the cemetery *(Camí del Cementeri)* also leads also leads past the

---

★ **Santa Maria**
You can admire the marvellous organ in this church in Maó
→ p. 40

★ **Tour of Port de Maó**
Cruise by glass-bottom boat through the Mediterranean's largest natural harbour
→ p. 43

★ **Cales Coves**
The twin bay with its 100 caves has an eventful past → p. 49

★ **Binibèquer Vell**
Fascinating warren of narrow alleys with lots of nooks and crannies: resort design of the future → p. 50

MARCO POLO HIGHLIGHTS

turn-off to Cala Sant Esteve to the ruins of the fortress which once guarded the entrance to Port de Maó. Spain's King Philip II saw only one means of defence against the constant threat from pirates: the construction of a fortification. Building started in 1554. The British later extended it into one of the most secure fortifications in the Mediterranean. It was considered so secure that, on his accession, Charles III ordered its destruction. Today you can see ruins, where nature is slowly but surely taking over again, underground tunnels and corridors *(June– Sept Thu and Sun 10am 2-hour guided tours, otherwise only with pre-booking | admission 5 euros, night visit by torchlight 20 euros | tel. 9 71 36 21 00 | www.museo militarmenorca.com/san-felipe)*.

Another fortress protects the southern shore of the nearby *Cala Sant Esteve*. The British built *Fort Marlborough (see p. 107)* here in the 18th century and today, as a museum, it provides a trip back into the past.

ILLA DEL LLATZERET (131 E–F4) *(∅ K6)*

The name says it all: "Hospital island" – strategically located directly at the harbour entrance – was home to the largest hospital in the Mediterranean. From 1817–1917 this was the port quarantine centre. Heavily guarded and protected by massive walls, this hospital cared for patients with infectious diseases, such as the victims of the 1821 yellow fever and tetanus epidemic. In addition to the hospital, which is today used as a spa hotel for officials and as a congress venue, there is a small *museum*. You can reach "hospital island" by boat from Es Castell as part of a two-and-a-half-hour tour (in English) *(June–Oct Thu, Sun 5–7.30pm, Sat 10am–12.30pm | tour 18 euros | laza retodemahon.es)*; INSIDER TIP cultural events such as open-air film showings and concerts are often held here *(www. nanventura.es)*.

MAÓ

MAP INSIDE BACK COVER

(131 E4) *(∅ J6)* **With a population of only 29,000, Menorca's capital may be small but it is in fact home to approximately half the island's inhabitants. Sitting pretty on one of the world's best natural harbours, Maó is built atop the cliffs with the fjord-like bay below and its pretty villas and Colonial style houses give the city its particular charm.**

Maó has much to offer in the way of culture with some of Menorca's best museums, Spain's oldest opera house and several churches. The city also has a long line of bars, restaurants and clubs to choose from along its regenerated quayside. It's worth spending a few days in Maó to get to know the capital's inhabitants. The next beaches are just a few miles away and all of the island's resorts are easily accessible by bus or car.

Maó is divided into three distinct parts: the historic centre is in the upper part of the city from where you can head down to the "down at the sea" district (Baixamar) with its line of restaurants and amusements along the quayside. "On the other side" (S'Altra Banda), i.e. on the fjord's north banks, you'll find more attractions. Most visitors first head to the Plaça de s'Esplanada with its bus station, car park and tourist information. The Carrer de ses Moreres on the east-side of the square takes you to the Plaça d'Espanya with a set of steps leading down to the harbour. Alternatively you can take the INSIDER TIP free lift next to the hotel *Port Mahon*.

SIGHTSEEING

ATENEU CIENTÌFIC (U A2) *(🗺 a2)*

The culture centre with the warm wooden and geometrically tiled floors is used by the Menorcans for *tertulias* – relaxed social gatherings. Holidaymakers are more

and good medical provision were amongst the benefits of the port channel three miles long and more than 1000 m/3300 ft wide. When necessary the port basin could be sealed off by means of a fortress *(Sant Felip)* – from the military point of view, the perfect

The party people on Maó's quayside get going when the sun begins to set

interested in the small exhibitions of ceramics, antique maps and fossils. The concerts and cinema club are also interesting. *Sun–Fri 10am–2pm, 4pm–9pm, in summer only mornings | Sa Rovellada de Dalt 25 | near Pl. de S'Esplanada | www. ateneumao.org*

BAIXAMAR (PORT) (U A–E1) *(🗺 a–e1)*

"Julio, agosto y Maó/los mejores puertos del Mediterraneo son" (July, August and Maó are the safest ports in the Mediterranean). At least this was the rhyme made up by someone who should know: Admiral Andrea Doria. He spoke only in glowing terms of his favourite port: adequate draught, excellent protection from wind and weather for a whole fleet,

port, unique for its size in the Mediterranean.

It is only in more recent times that the landlubbers of Maó have found more civilian uses for the port. It is now for pleasure that you go "down to the sea" to *Baixamar*. The port promenade offers not only an ever increasing range of food and drink, but also a variety of water sport activities, and a broad range of entertainment options. During the day there are souvenir shops, boat trips and the *Xoriguer* gin distillery, famous throughout the island; and then in the evening there are countless nightclubs, bars and pubs, many of them in the former warehouses and boat sheds, where you can spend time late into the night.

Baixamar is, however, not only the spruced up area around the two harbour breakwaters – *Moll de Ponent* lying to the west which extends east to the *Moll de Llevant*– but also the stretch of coast to the north and opposite. This is home to large industrial companies, warehouses and business premises as well as freight ship ter-

ists ⚜ INSIDER TIP Great views from the tower! *Tue–Sun 10am–1.30pm, Thu and Sat also 6–8pm | admission 5 euros, free on Sundays | C/ Anuncivay 2*

MOLÍ DEL REI ● ⊗ ⚜ (U C2) (*m̄ c2*)

The "King's mill" is a mill tower dating from the 18th century, that is being used

Civilised idleness in Maó's old town

minals; unfortunately, Menorca's only power station also belches emissions here, as well, which provides part of the island with energy – the rest coming via undersea cable from Mallorca.

CENTRE D'ART I D'HISTORIA HERNÁNDEZ SANZ (U C2) (*m̄ c2*)

Adorned with decorative murals, this restored merchants' house (1805) is a fine example of how Menorca's upper class once lived on the island. Besides its architecture, this museum houses an interesting collection, tracking the development of the harbour under British rule as well as exhibiting expressive paintings and etchings from Menorcan art-

as an ecological information centre, as a shop for Menorcan souvenirs (usually environmentally friendly), and above all as one of the best viewing platforms overlooking the old town and the port. *Mon–Fri 9.30am–2.30pm and Mon–Thu 5.30pm–8pm | admission free | Camí des Castell 53 | www.gobmenorca.com/moli*

MUSEU DE MENORCA ● (U A1) (*m̄ a1*)

A former monastery now full of treasures: In the *Sant Francesc* convent there are exhibits of archaeological finds, historic paintings and maps as well as ethnological items and contemporary art – Menorca's richest collection of traditions, customs, history and prehistory. You can also visit the picturesque cloister of the former Franciscan convent, whose origins date back to the 15th century. *June–Sept Tue–Sat 10am–2pm, 6pm–8pm, Sun 10am–2pm, Oct–May Tue, Thu 10am–6pm, Wed, Fri–Sun 10am–2pm | admission free | Placa Pla des Monestir | www.museudemenorca.com*

PLAÇA BASTIÓ (U B1–2) (*Ɱ b1–2*)

From the bars and cafés, you'll spot a gate flanked by towers – formerly part of the city's medieval wall. It used to be the starting point of a long journey to Ciutadella, the western peak of the island, but today, anyone who wants to head to the nearby bus station has to pass through it.

PLAÇA DEL CARME (U B–C2) (*Ɱ b–c2*)

This is one spot everyone passes: Maó's central square is named after the former *Claustre del Carme* convent whose colonnades (erected from 1726) house souvenir and delicatessen shops as well as some vegetable and fruit stands. Most produce is now sold in the modern basement, where there is a supermarket -- the locals buy their groceries here (*www.mercatdesclaustre.com,* parking garage on the Plaça Miranda). The *Mercat des Peix*, the fish market between Plaça del Carme and Plaça d'Espanya, offers all the bounty of the sea. Try to arrive as early as you can to get the best selection. The little tapas bars and the beautiful views of the harbour below are another attraction here (*Tue–Sat from 7.30am*).

PLAÇA DE LA CONQUESTA (U B1) (*Ɱ b1*)

Here, in the oldest part of the town, is the cultural centre *Casa de Cultura* with an informative public library and the town archive; a few steps further on is the *town hall* (construction began in 1789). From the

end of the short alleyway *Carrer d'Alfons III* you can enjoy a lovely ☀ **INSIDER TIP** panoramic view over the port.

PLAÇA DE S'ESPLANADA (U A2) (*Ɱ a2*)

If you arrive by bus, this will be the starting point for your exploration of Maó: From Plaça de S'Esplanada, *Carrer de ses Moreres* leads eastwards into the old part of the town – lined with terrace bars and traditional shops. You'll also see a bronze bust of one of Maó's illustrious residents: Dr Mateu Orfila (1787–1853), famous among physicians as the father of toxicology, the study of poisons.

At the end of the boulevard, *Carrer Bastió* forks off to the left, and if you go to the right it leads to *Costa d'en Deia* and *Plaça Reial* with the town's theatre, the *Teatro Principal*. Facing straight ahead, you would be looking at the town gate through which Ottoman corsair Hayreddin Barbarossa once forced his way into Maó before subjugating and plundering the town and abducting more than 1000 inhabitants. A dramatic footnote: a very

LOW BUDGET

At nearly all the museums on the island, university students and senior citizens receive a discount – but make sure to bring your ID!

In Maó, you can spend the night at the *Residencia Jume* (U C2) (*Ɱ c2*) (*39 rooms | C/ Concepció 4–6 | tel. 9 71 36 32 66 | www.hostaljume.com*) from 60 euros for a double; it's centrally located in the old town, clean and respectable – popular among younger guests from the Spanish mainland.

Miraculous pipes: Even human voices emerge from the Santa Maria organ

small number of the merchants are said to have opened the gate for the pirates in order to protect their own property. From the Plaça heading north you come to the capital's bus station.

SANTA MARIA ★ (U B1) (*🗺 b1*)

Construction of the Santa Maria parish church was started in 1748 on the ruins of an older chapel. Rather simple at first glance, Santa Maria appeals more to the ear than the eye because inside is a INSIDER TIP masterpiece of organ building. In 1809 a commission was placed with the German-Swiss organ builders Otter & Kyburz and the instrument was delivered to Menorca in just one year. With its 3120 pipes and four manuals it was soon well-known throughout the island, especially for its ability to imitate the human voice. The organ looks stunning from up close on the first floor. *Mon–Sat 9am–12.30pm, 3.30pm–7pm, 30 min. organ recital June–Oct Mon–Sat 1pm | admission to concert 5 euros, church 2 euros | between Plaça de la Conquesta and Plaça de la Constitució*

SANT FRANCESC (U A1) (*🗺 a1*)

The people of Maó also call this church the "cathedral". It took almost a century to build (1719–92), which is reflected in the mix of architectural styles. Next to it is the former Franciscan convent *Sant Francesc* founded in 1439, today the *Museu de Menorca*. The road there is lined with stately buildings. *Plaça des Monestir*

BAIXAMAR (U A1) (*🗺 a1*)

Modernismo (Spanish Art Nouveau) is the theme of this quayside café with its black and white tiles, dark wooden furniture and illuminating mirrors. Every generation and class of people meet up here at all times of the day and night in Maó. *Daily from 9am | Moll de Ponent 17 | Budget*

LA CAVA DEL ARS ● (U C2) (⌘ c2)

This is a cosy café on the ground floor of a stately old sandstone house, furnished in a homely style and with Thonet chairs and bistro tables. It is mostly locals who come here to enjoy good wines and, at lunchtimes and in the evenings, the homemade tapas. In the *La Cava* cellar vaults you can enjoy live concerts and club nights *(from 11.30pm)*. *Mon–Thu 9am–midnight, Fri/Sat 9am–4am | Plaça Princep 12 | tel. 9 71 35 18 79 | arscafe. wordpress.com/el-cafe | Moderate*

MERCAT DES PEIX (U B–C2) (⌘ b–c2)

Centrally located, but well hidden: The fish market at the front sells all the bounty of the sea, while the line of tapas bars at the back serve Menorcan specialties: mussels caught in the fjord, sausages and cheeses produced inland and delicate sweet pastries. *Mon–Sat 11.30am–3pm, 7.30pm–11pm | between Plaça del Carme and Plaça d'Espanya | Budget–Moderate*

NAUTIC LOUNGE (O) (⌘ O)

A truly unique culinary experience! Take a seat in a small round boat with a BBQ built up in the centre and sail around and explore the harbour while your food is cooking on the grill (no yachting licence required). There are different menus to choose from, ranging from BBQ to sushi. *Starts around noon and in the evening | 300 Moll de Llevant | mobile 6 09 30 04 59 | www.nauticlounge.com | Expensive*

RESTAURANTE PIZZERÍA ROMA (O) (⌘ O)

This is probably Maó's most popular pizzeria, with reasonable prices, impeccable view of the port and an international ambience. Its reasonably priced lunchtime and evening menus (the latter only served off season) offer a variety of dishes: just ask Señor Enric what he recommends. *Daily | Moll de Llevant 295 | tel. 9 71 35 37 77 | www.restaurantepizzeri aroma.com | Budget–Moderate*

FOR BOOKWORMS & FILM BUFFS

The Life of Richard Kane – by Bruce Laurie, a serious academic study of Britain's first governor of Menorca presents a fascinating picture of life on the island in the 18th century, only available in hardback.

Plants of the Balearic Islands – by Anthony Bonner, this indispensable pocket guide to the marvellous flora of the islands is now available in an excellent new edition. For the non-expert, it is ideal if you simply want to know what you are looking at as you stroll through the countryside.

Isla Bonita – The light-hearted Fernando Colomo comedy was filmed on Menorca in 2016. It's about a director having a mid-life crisis against the backdrop of beautiful nature – mottled light, crystal-clear water, captivating green

Walk! Menorca – by David and Ros Brawn, a comprehensive guide to walks in Menorca with ratings for distance, time etc. There are clear maps and photos. But buy it before you go because it is not available in Menorca

SES FORQUILLES (U A2) (*m a2*)

Oriol and Raquel's young team serve tasty, nicely presented dishes with a creative touch. Their speciality is Menorcan king prawns with smoke and truffles. Also tapas in a lively bistro atmosphere. *Closed Tue and Wed evenings and Sun | Rovellada de Dalt 20 | tel. 9 71 35 27 11 | www.sesforquilles.com | Moderate*

SHOPPING

Carrer Hannóver (U B2) (*m b2*) or – as the Menorcans prefer – *Costa de Sa Plaça*, is Maó's shopping street. Lined with palm trees and paved with cobblestones, *Plaça Colon* offers welcome variety. This and *Carrer Nou* are the places to meet for a celebration or just a cup of coffee. A lovely *market* (including arts and crafts) is held on *Tue and Sat 9am–2pm* on *Plaça de S'Esplanada* (U A2) (*m a2*). The night market *Mercat de Nit* (U B–C2) (*m b–c2*) (*July/Aug Tue 8–11pm | Plaça del Carmen*) is even more attractive.

S'ALAMBIC (U B1) (*m b1*)

You can buy typical Menorcan souvenirs here in a typical Menorcan building: ceramics, costume jewellery, clothing and leather goods. *Moll de Ponent 36*

INSIDER TIP AUTÈNTIC (U A2) (*m a2*)

Between the bus station and the Hannóver high street, you'll find authentic Menorcan treats: Chamomile liqueur, wine, gin and pomada, cheese, sausage, and sweets. Try before you buy! A friendly señor will tell you all about the products and neatly gift-wrap your souvenirs. *Plaça Explanada 13*

DESTILERÍA GIN XORIGUER (U A1) (*m a1*)

You can get Gin Xoriguer in almost every bar and restaurant in Menorca. But here in Maós port is where it is produced and can be sampled. You can buy it in decorative glass or clay bottles. Try the herbal liqueurs, too! To this very day the Pons family keeps the secret of the key ingredients under lock and key. Around 60 per cent of production is consumed on the island as *pomada* or neat. *Andén de Poniente 91 (branch in the old town: Plaça del Carme 16) | www.xoriguer.es*

JAIME MASCARÓ (U A2) (*m a2*)

Well-known shoe brands, all made locally, with unusual styles; they also sell belts and bags. *C/ Ses Moreres 29 | www.jaimemascaro.es*

LA MARVILLA (U B1–2) (*m b1–2*)

Nice, small gift shop in the centre. They have something rather special: the friendly looking Menorcan mule neighing out at you from cups, aprons and T-shirts. *C/ Portal del Mar 7*

PONS QUINTANA (U B2) (*m b2*)

Here you will find some rather wacky women's shoes: from pink pumps to turquoise cowboy boots. *C/ S'Arravaleta 21 | www.ponsquintana.com*

SUCRERÍA CA'N VALLÉS (U B2) (*m b2*)

This is where the connoisseurs reckon you can get the best *ensaïmadas* in town, also other tasty dishes typical of the island. *C/ Hannóver 16*

INSIDER TIP EL TURRONERO (U B2) (*m b2*)

If you are looking for edible Menorcan souvenirs, then you have struck gold here. The range of products includes not only sweets *(turrones)* and excellent ice cream, but also cheese and cold meats. *C/ Nou 22–24*

SPORTS & ACTIVITIES

BOAT TRIPS

Strolling down Maó's promenades is wonderful, but experiencing the city from the water is even more exhilarating. The one-hour ★ *port cruise in Maó* focuses on Port de Maó and is a must for every holiday-

Canutells, with breaks for a swim in summer *(in summer daily 10am and 2.30pm, return approx. 1pm or 5.30pm).*

SAILING

From these companies in Maó you can book sailing trips and hire boats: *Menorca Náutica (Moll de Llevant 163 | tel.*

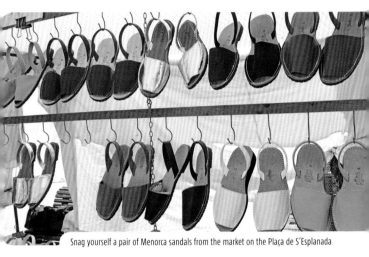
Snag yourself a pair of Menorca sandals from the market on the Plaça de S'Esplanada

maker on Menorca. INSIDER TIP Get an early start to avoid the crowds! Boats depart from the port steps (close to the ferry terminal). The ship "Don Joan" by *Líneas de la Cruz (during summer several cruises daily Mon–Sat | ticket 12 euros | tickets tel. 9 71 35 07 78 | rutasmaritimas delacruz.com)* will sail you around the natural harbour for an hour, while you look through the underwater windows and listen to the commentary. *Líneas de la Cruz* also organises half-day excursions to remote bays and beaches, some of which are otherwise inaccessible. Tours start from Maó and head north-east via Sa Mesquida to Illa d'en Colom and the Es Grau Nature Reserve as well as south via Punta Prima and Binibèquer to

9 71 35 45 43 | www.menorcanautic.com), Blue Mediterraneum (Moll de Llevant | mobile tel. 6 09 30 52 14), Menorca Cruising School (CMoll de Levant 303 | Sant Lluis | mobile tel. 6 60 64 78 45 | www. menorcasailing.co.uk | also sailing lessons)

TENNIS

Tennis court with floodlight: *Tenis Mahón (C/ Trepucó 4 | tel. 9 71 36 05 76)*

ENTERTAINMENT

INSIDER TIP *Nits de Música al Carrer* is a thrilling event; every Tuesday evening in summer *(late June–late Aug., 9–11.30 pm)*, many shops are open after official hours, restaurants offer cheap tapas, and live bands deliver the perfect backdrop of sound, from funk or fusion to flamenco. There are lots of things also for young people to do in the western port area around *Moll de Ponent* – bars, cafés and pubs that all cater for night owls. The ones most popular with locals are the cosy *Baixamar* (see "Food & Drink") and the jazz and dance club *Akelarre (Thu often live performances | Moll de Ponent 42 | www.facebook.com/akelarrejazzdance)* with cocktails and trendy clientele.

The eastern port district round *Moll de Llevant* has a more sedate and international feel. One institution is *Bar Nou (C/ Nou 1)*. Housed in an art nouveau building in the upper part of the city close to the Santa Maria church, this bar serves cocktails in a quiet, vintage setting with a pretty outside seating area. Nightlife in Maó can also be found in *Assukar (Sun–Thurs from 8pm, Fri/Sat from 10pm | C/ Francesc Borja Moll)* which plays salsa and other Latin beats. A mix of theme parties,

DJ sessions and live concerts is held at this venue and its terrace is a good place to enjoy a refreshing drink to cool down. On the edge of the old town is the *Cristiano i Gradinata (C/ Isabel II.)* bar with fantastic views over the city and where Señor Chiqi has a preference for jazz and blues: the ⚜ INSIDER TIP *Mirador des ses Monges* is just a few steps away where the city's harbour spreads out below you. This is a popular meeting point for locals. If you're looking for something in the way of culture, don't miss out on a concert at the ● *Teatre (Costa Deia 40 | www.teatremao. com)* Spain's oldest opera house offers amazing architecture and acoustics.

WHERE TO STAY

CASA ALBERTI ⚜ (U B2) (*ⓜ b2*)
Feel at home in this noble palace dating from 1740. Situated in one of the prettiest corners of the old town, climb the hotel's marble staircase to the spacious, high-ceilinged rooms, which are all furnished

A must for fans of classic: a concert in Maó's theatre house

with antique furniture. Breakfast emphasises local produce and offers the perfect start to your day. The owner welcomes her guests like she would her friends. There is even an honesty fridge in the bar where guests can help themselves during the day (and write down what they have spent). The rooftop terrace offers a panoramic view of the region around. *7 rooms | C/ Isabel II. 9 | tel. 6 86 39 35 69 | www.casalberti.com | Moderate*

INSIDER TIP ▶ **JARDI DE SES BRUIXES**
(U C2) (*⌖ c2*)
This elegant historic building was constructed in 1812; 100 years later, it was renovated in art nouveau style, and another 100 years later, the current owner – an architect – gave it a trendy makeover. The rooms at Ses Bruixes are individually decorated, each one with its own charm, original architectural features and exceptional bathrooms, some of which are integrated into the rooms (free WiFi, fireplace). The continental breakfast is served in the romantic courtyard café – *al estilo menorquín* on request. *7 rooms | C/ de Sant Ferrán 26 | Tel. 9 71 36 31 66 | www.hotelsesbruixes.com | Moderate*

PORT MAHÓN ☆☆ (0) (*⌖ 0*)
The island capital's most prestigious hotel, a four-star establishment offering fantastic views over the sea and the marina. It is fully renovated and sumptuously furnished, with air conditioning, swimming pool and mini bar. *82 rooms | Av. Port de Maó 13 | tel. 9 71 36 26 00 | www.sethotels.com | Expensive*

INFORMATION

OFICINA D'INFORMACIÓ TURÍSTICA
(U B2) (*⌖ b2*)
Plaça Constitució 22 | town hall | tel. 9 71 36 37 90 | www.menorca.es , www.

ajmao.org | branch at the harbour: Mull de Llevant 2 | tel. 9 71 35 59 52

BUSES

Several times daily to Ciutadella *(bus station Pl. de S'Esplanada)*; information: *mobile tel. 9 71 36 04 75* (in Spanish) or at the tourist information. There are other regular connections from Maó to Es Castell, Sant Lluís, Es Migjorn Gran and Sant Tomàs, Ferreries and Cala Galdana, Sant Climent and Cala En Porter, to Alaior and Son Bou, Fornells and Arenal d'en Castell.

WHERE TO GO

ILLA DEL REI (131 E4) (*⌖ J–K6*)
Governor Kane commissioned the construction of the huge hospital complex which to this day covers a major part of the small island in the Port de Maó bay. Since its construction in the 18th century until the 1950s, the building was used as a hospital. The island, which British seafarers 200 years ago christened *Bloody Island,* is shrouded in dark tales, and surgical waste is said to have been thrown into the sea in days gone by. In 1986 the Maó town council announced the building was to be used to establish a public institution and there was talk of a genetic research centre and of a museum; Elton John wanted to take up residence there; the Balearic Electricity Works wanted to establish a research facility; and speculators wanted to build a hotel. But to this day the building still stands empty. The remains of an early Christian basilica are to be found on Illa del Rei, though its main attraction, a relatively well preserved mosaic, is exhibited in the *Museu de Menorca* in Maó. The small island owes its name to Alfonso III of Aragon who landed there in 1287 and held out until reinforcements arrived to

re-take Menorca from the hands of the Moorish occupying forces. *2.5-hour tour from Maó Moll de Levant April–Sept only Sun 8.45am and 10.45am with the "Yellow Submarine" | ticket 7 euros | www. islahospitalmenorca.org*

LA MOLA ● ☄ (131 F4) (*Ⓜ K6*)

Both the French and British occupiers of the island considered transforming the strategically important peninsula at the entrance to the bay of Maó into a bastion. However, the present fortress complex was constructed from 1850–60, after the demolition of the castle of San Felipe by the Spaniards. On the occasion of an in-auguration, Queen Isabella II of Bourbon visited the fort, which was subsequently given the name "Fortalesa Isabel II". In 1930 the facilities were once again up-graded and two Vickers Armstrong guns were installed. However, the fortress was never involved in military conflicts, which is why it is so perfectly preserved and offers a variety of activities. The activities include guided tours *(6 euros)*, bike rides, jeep safaris *(14.50 euros)* as well as con-certs and theatre and dance performanc-es. You will find the current events calen-dar at: *www.fortalesalamola.com. Access via Port de Maó, Carretera La Mola, 7 km/5 miles | May–Sep 10am–8pm, Oct and April 10am–6pm, Nov–March 10am–2pm | ad-mission 8 euros*

SA MESQUIDA (131 E3) (*Ⓜ J–K5*)

This is where the people of Maó come to swim and sunbathe. The 700 m/765 yds coastline is divided into two parts by a headland. The larger beach is around 300 m/328 yds long, but is not well suited for children as the ground falls away quite steeply. Sa Mesquida was also the start-ing point in 1781 of the Franco-Spanish reconquest, which gave the British reason enough to secure the bay with its own

fortification (1798). Restaurant tip: *Cap Roig (April–Oct daily | C/ de Sa Mesquida 13 | tel. 9 71 18 83 83 | Budget–Moderate)*, inviting terrace overlooking the sea.

TALAIOT DE TREPUCÓ ● (131 E4) (*Ⓜ J6*)

The prehistoric settlement situated 2 km/ 1.2 mile south of Maó is often described as the site with the most spectacular megalith in the Balearics, the *taula* (more than 4.20 m/13 ft high), and with the largest *talaiot* construction (40 m/131 ft diameter). It's believed that the settle-ment was founded sometime around 1700 B.C. and extended far beyond the "holy shrine". Today, you can still see the remnants of the settlement beyond the enclosing wall. *Admission free*

TALATÍ DE DALT (131 D4) (*Ⓜ H6*)

You'll find the ruins of this ancient settle-ment in a windswept landscape of olive and fig trees. Climb over the enclosing wall to feel like you've been transported back to an era when animals were sacri-ficed on the enormous *taula* supported by stone slabs. The animals were likely kept in the caves, which they entered via large openings. Access is signposted (main road Maó–Ciutadella, 4 km/2.5 miles). *10am–sunset | admission 4 euros | www.disfrutamenorca.com/talati-de-dalt*

SANT CLIMENT

(131 D4) (*Ⓜ H6*) **On your way to the southern coast, you'll pass this small town 10 km southwest of Maó.**

If it weren't for the nearby airport, you might think you were in the countryside. But there aren't many planes taking off and landing in Menorca, so the Menorcan middle class have built lovely houses for

Just a crumbling wall? Nope! Prehistoric settlement ruins in Talatí de Dalt

themselves in this idyllic area. You should have a look at the *Basílica des Fornas de Torelló* with a mosaic dating from the 6th century and the *Talaiot de Torelló* (both to the left of the Sant Climent–Maó main road, just before the turn off to the airport). The remarkable *Curnia* estate with elements of art nouveau is not far away; it is said to have been designed by a pupil of Gaudí. There is another *talaiot (Talaiot de Curnia | 2.8k m/1.7 mile)* behind the main building.

FOOD & DRINK

ES MOLÍ DE FOC
Dinner at a mill? Good international cuisine with French influences in a pleasant atmosphere in the restored mill. In-house brewery. *Daily | C/ Sant Llorenç 65 | tel. 9 71 15 32 22 | www.esmolidefoc.es | Moderate*

INSIDER TIP RESTAURANTE CASINO SANT CLIMENT
Here you can enjoy an evening meal in a typical British atmosphere; there are jazz sessions on Tuesdays in summer from 8.30pm. *Daily | C/ Sant Jaume 4 | tel. 9 71 15 34 18 | www.casinosantcliment. com | Expensive*

SHOPPING

You will find food and bakery products on the Sant Jaume thoroughfare, and Bernardo Pons' homemade cheese *(Quesos de Sant Climent)* in the C/ Sant Llorenç.

WHERE TO GO

CALA EN PORTER (130 B–C4) (*M G6*)
On the left (as you look from the sea) everything's still in a natural state, whereas on the right there is a holiday resort

that extends up the slope. The beach at the end of the bay is 400 m/437 yds wide, with fine sand sloping down gently to the sea – ideal for the whole family. Be aware, however, that the word is out!

A first-rate attraction is the nightclub with café ✲ *Cova d'en Xoroi (May–Sept daily 11.30am–9.30pm | admission incl. drink 11am–4.30pm 9 euros, 13 euros after 5pm | C/ de Sa Cova 2 | tel. 9 71 37 72 36 | www.covadenxoroi.com)* in a natural grotto. Location, view and atmosphere are unique. Halfway between sea and sky, on the steep slopes of the coastal cliffs, it provides a breath-taking view of the sea. It's particularly beautiful at sunset.

The cliffs glow in the golden light, and far below, a fishing boat chugs by; the

Disco with thrill factor: Cova d'en Xoroi

seagulls sailing across the sky are practically close enough to touch. And when night falls, the themed parties begin – from dolce vita to hippie chic.

No wonder that this place has become something of a legend. The Moor pirate Xoroi (the one-eared), who was left behind by his crew on the coast of Menorca after a raid, is said to have used it as a base. Word spread amongst the peasants that there was a bandit in hiding: one day hens were missing, the next day a pig. And then one day a beautiful young peasant girl disappeared. The peasants only discovered the thief's hiding place years later when, one winter's night, some snow had fallen on the fields and footprints led them to the cave. The armed peasants stormed the pirate's cave and he hurled himself into the sea. They found the young woman in the best of health and with three children... A few kilometres inland, the hotel *Torralbenc (22 rooms | Ctra. Maó–Cala en Porter, km 10 | tel. 9 71 37 72 11 | www.torralbenc. com | Expensive)* is also an attraction: The estate sits on a hillside, surrounded by vineyards. The rooms are furnished with natural materials, and there is a lovely pool garden from where you can overlook the landscape and the sea. Creative Menorcan cuisine is served in the restaurant.

But the region's top restaurant is the INSIDER**TIP** ▶ *Brasserie & Bar Dos Pablos (May–Oct daily from 6.30am | C/ de la Mediterrània 3 | tel. 9 71 37 79 12 | www.facebook.com/brasseriebardospa blos | Moderate–Expensive)*. The British owners break down all the stereotypes about English cuisine: They conjure up delicious dishes that even produce appreciative "Oohs" and "Aahs" from dyed-in-the-wool Menorcans, and they come up with inventive new recipes every year.

CALES COVES ★ ● (130 B–C4) (*Ⓜ G6*)

Where 3000 years ago the original inhabitants buried their dead, there lived a clan of latter day hippies until the middle of the 1990s. The place name (cave bays) is in the plural because the bay is divided into two areas of land, in one of which there is a freshwater spring; both bury deeply into the greyish brown rock. Well protected from the wind, the water in the bay is calm and crystal clear, but access via a gravel path is very uneven. A more enjoyable route is to follow the red-signposted GR-223 trail from Cala en Porter on foot *(start at the Mirador; the hike takes approx. 1.40 hr one way)*.

The caves total about 100 and have a complex past. The oldest date from the 11th century BC and were used as burial sites. Up to the 4th century BC larger caves were dug into the limestone rock, often with a central supporting column, benches and niches, also used as burial sites. Even Roman traces have been found. Some of the caves were used for ritual purposes and seafarers – also buccaneers – and fishermen repeatedly used the bay as a shelter in rough seas.

ES CANUTELLS (130 C5) (*Ⓜ G–H7*)

For the inhabitants of Sant Climent the bay is their town "port". It's lovely on the water, where the boathouses carved into the cliffs and a set of weathered stairs leading to the small beach stand as reminders of a Menorca from a bygone era. In recent years a resort has developed above the bay extending deep into the interior; only the western edge of the bay has so far been largely spared. On the road from Sant Climent to Sant Lluís, you can still admire a lovely example of Menorcan hybrid architecture: the manor *Casat de Formet (Forma Vell)* from the 19th century impresses with its red facade and beautiful, terraced garden with fountains and other water features.

SANT LLUÍS

(131 E5) (*Ⓜ J7*) Another "Sant" – a saint – in a city name! To honour its patron, Sant Lluís, this town is immaculately clean: The buildings are painted white and are neat as a pin, the roads are well-maintained, and things are almost too tranquil.

If the town's name sounds French to you, you're absolutely right: Count Lannion, governor when the island was under French rule, founded the place on a flying visit in the 18th century, designing it with pencil and ruler with the result that the town's layout is geometrical. The church which gave the place its name was dedicated to the French King Louis IX. Today, foreigners and people fleeing their hectic lives in Maó are most likely to settle here, which is why the city has a number of excellent restaurants. In the restored *mill (Mon–Sat 10am–1pm and 6–9pm | free admission)* at the northern entrance to the town, you can learn more about the traditional milling industry.

FOOD & DRINK

INSIDER TIP PAN Y VINO

The 200-year-old country estate in the hamlet of Torret (on the way to the coast) is pure relaxation: Enjoy creative Mediterranean-Menorcan cuisine and – thanks to Patrick and Noelia – top-notch service in this elegant, modern country home atmosphere (even on the terrace). Sometimes there's live music, with a jazz band performing in the evening. *Closed Tue and during lunchtime | Camí de la Coixa 3 (Torret) | towards Punta Prima, km*

6 | tel. 9 71 15 03 22 | www.panyvinome
norca.com | *Expensive*

INSIDER TIP SA PEDRERA D'ES PUJOL

This cosy restaurant in Torret features light
sandstone walls reminiscent of an old
quarry; Daniel and Nuria serve up original
dishes. Their creative cuisine is rounded
off by an extensive wine list. *Daily | Camí
des Pujol 14 | towards Punta Prima, km 6 |
tel. 9 71 15 07 17 | www.sapedreradespujol.
com | Expensive*

INSIDER TIP LA RUEDA

Cheap tapas and set menus – no wonder
it is often packed here around noon.
Simple furnishings, noisy, good vibes!
*Closed Tue | C/ Sant Lluis 30 | tel.
9 71 15 03 49 | Moderate*

WHERE TO STAY

INSIDER TIP BINIARROCA COUNTRY HOTEL

Dating from the 18th century, this country house is owned by Sheelagh Ratliff, a
former London fashion designer. She has
transformed the property into a stylish retreat and entertains guests by providing
lots of tips! Attractive garden with two
pools entwined with bougainvillea; the
romantic restaurant serves sophisticated,
French-inspired cuisine. *18 rooms | Camí
Vell 57; 2 km/1.8 mile from Sant Lluís | tel.
9 71 15 00 59 | www.biniarroca.com | Mod-
erate–Expensive*

INFORMATION

Town hall | C/ de Sant Lluís | tel.
9 71 15 09 50

WHERE TO GO

S'ALGAR (131 E5) (*[U] K7*)

No sandy beaches? That can be a good
thing! In this coastal town where you
climb down ladders from the rocks into
the water, mass tourism simply doesn't
exist, even in the high season. Rather
than broiling on the beach, try participat-
ing in some water sports – the choices
are nearly endless. *Club S'Algar Diving
(Passeig Marítin | tel. 9 71 15 06 01 | www.
salgardiving.com)*, the water sports centre, offers almost every type of water
sport. Here you can also hire diving equip-
ment and sailing boats. The *S'Algar Hotel
(106 rooms | tel. 9 71 15 17 00 | www.sal
garhotels.com | Expensive)* enjoys a good
reputation – it's cosy and sedate here,
and visitors love the food. It has no direct
access to the beach but has a fantastic
swimming pool with sea views. If you
fancy peace and quiet in a natural setting,
you can walk round the little cove *Cala
Rafalet* to the north at a height of 15–30
m (50–100 ft).

BINIBÈQUER VELL ⭐
(131 D5) (*[U] H–J7*)

The main tourist attraction on the south-
east coast of Menorca is reminiscent of a
rabbit warren. This "typical fishing village"
actually came off the architectural draw-
ing board in 1972, but the labyrinthine
passages, tunnels, junctions and alcoves
are so cleverly designed that they feel like
they've developed organically over the
centuries. Prior to the start of the season,
the complex sparkles in pristine white,
the natural stone floors are polished, souvenir shops and bars start to display their
offers in the windows. In peak season it
gets rather crowded in the narrow nooks
and crannies. You can enjoy tapas, fresh
fish and excellent chocolate cake in the
*Club Náutico (daily. | Passeig del Mar 29 |
near Hotel Eden, right by the sea | nauti
cobinisafua.com | Moderate)*; relaxed
atmosphere and superb sunsets. The
beach bar *Bucaneros (Platja de
Binibèquer | Budget)* is also an excellent

Stunning backdrop in radiant white: Binibèquer Vell

place to treat yourself to a cool beer under a bamboo umbrella. There's always live music at the full moon in the *Bar Paupa (Cala Torret | C/ de Platja de Llevant | Moderate)*.

CALA D'ALCALFAR (131 E5) (*Ø K7*)

This is how all the fishing villages on the island once looked. Cala d'Alcalfar (or Alcaufar) is a simple village, mainly used by Menorcans, with white boat houses by the sea. A natural breakwater at the entrance to the cove ensures a calm sea. Hotel tip: *Xuroy (46 rooms | tel. 9 71 15 18 20 | www.xuroymenorca.com | Budget)* on the edge of the village. The beach hotel is satisfactory and provides holidays away from the madding crowd.

PUNTA PRIMA (131 E6) (*Ø J7*)

Even from a distance, you can see the sea sparkling in an almost surreal turquoise colour. This attractive shade is the result of the white limestone; it lends the water its lovely colouring. The red and white lighthouse on the offshore *Illa de l'Aire*, the "island of the air", is the final glorious touch to this riot of colours. Take some

extra time to enjoy the beautiful view from the vantage point (indicated by a sign) on the west side of the bay (Punta de Mabres). Punta Prima has a wide beach of fine, white sand that gently drops down to the sea. It might not seem as romantic as other bays, but it's family-friendly, so it's popular and can be busy. At the *Occidental Menorca (374 rooms | C/ Mestral de Punta Prima | tel. 9 71 15 90 70 | www.barcelo.com | Expensive)* the emphasis is on families with children. For the younger guests there is an entertainment programme while parents can enjoy an elaborate spa area with jacuzzi, steam bath, sauna and hot stone massage. The five-star hotel *Insotel Punta Prima Prestige (52 rooms | C/ Mitjanera de Punta Prima | Sant Lluis | tel. 9 71 19 51 61 | www.insotelhotelgroup. com | Expensive)* oozes class: beautifully tended gardens, exquisite rooms, appealing architecture and an exclusive spa area with adjacent beauty and fitness centre all satisfy the most stringent demands. You can find the tourist information office on Passeig de s'Arenal *(www. ajsantlluis.org)*.

TRAMUNTANA/ NORTH

"The Tramuntana does not rest and does not forgive", says a Menorcan proverb, and when you see the bizarre shapes of the coastal cliffs – weathered by storm and spray over thousands of years – and the deformed pine trees bent by the northerly winds, you can immediately agree.

It also explains why hundreds of galleons and fishing boats have sunk in the course of history off the rugged coast between Punta Nati and Cap de Favàritx, and why the people on the north coast tend to be rather quiet and introspective, because the *Tramuntana* shapes not only rock and wood, but also the inhabitants. And so, from time immemorial, psychological influences have been ascribed to this occasionally stiff north wind, and re-cently medical statistics have proven the link between the wind and a ten-dency towards depression. Nevertheless, some of Menorca's most beautiful, un-spoilt and quietest natural beaches are here: Cala Tirant, Port d'Addaia, Arenal de Son Saura, Cala Pregonda, Na Macaret...

FORNELLS

(128 B–C2) (*ℳ G2*) Here even the Spanish royal family occasionally en-joys a *caldereta* (lobster in vegetable stock), which is particularly well made in ⭐ Fornells. And the setting is perfect too: a lovely, quiet lagoon on the other-wise rugged northern coast with the old

Rugged, green north: where the constant wind shapes both the landscape and the nature of the people

fishing port whose inhabitants enjoy a reputation as the best lobster fishermen in the western Mediterranean.
In this context "best" doesn't only refer to the size of the catch – the superb seafood is grilled daily in all the local pubs or dropped into the clay pot – but also to their careful management of the *langosta*, because the fishing season is limited to between April and August. And a further feature which has left its mark on Fornells (pop. 1000): in the 1960s the Norwegian artist Arnulf Björndal settled in Fornells and opened the island's first art gallery in the town centre (subsequently turned into a bar). Other artists followed, mainly Scandinavian and Spanish, resulting in an eclectic artistic community.
Fornells itself dates from back to the 17th century. When King Philip IV had a small fortress erected at the entrance to the bay in 1625, fishermen and their families as well as the accompanying priest soon settled in a row of houses. The fortress and the church were not able to resist

the march of time – the present church is much younger, dating from the 18th century.

SIGHTSEEING

SA TORRE DE FORNELLS ⚘

This was the island's most important defence tower, as its extremely massive design makes abundantly clear; it was

Surf school in Fornells: a good place for beginners

one of 164 defence towers on Menorca, . which the British erected primarily as a defence against their French opponents in the western Mediterranean. Today, it offers a spectacular view of the coast and lagoon. A small multimedia show and the tower itself provide insights into the defence of an island. *May–Oct Tue–Sun 11am–2pm, 5–8pm | admission 2.50 euros*

FOOD & DRINK

ES CRANC

"The Crab" is not located directly on the seafront but is still a popular destination.

Ask about prices before ordering though as you will only be handed a menu if you ask for one. Tasty fish dishes, good *calderetas*, efficient service. *Daily | C/ Escoles 31 | tel. 9 71 37 64 42 | Expensive*

LA GUAPA ●

"The Beauty" is a small, modest restaurant serving Mediterranean home cooking. Enjoy prawns in garlic oil as a starter, followed by a paella or maybe a Menorcan crayfish *caldereta?* Ask the waiter for tips on which ingredients were delivered fresh that day! *Closed Mon | C/ Major 29 | tel. 9 71 15 84 97 | Moderate–Expensive*

SPORTS & ACTIVITIES

BOAT TRIPS

Excursions to *Marina Norte,* the marine nature reserve to the west of Fornells, are subject to strict control. *Aventura Nàutica (Av. Passeig Marítim 41 | tel. 6 89 02 28 86 | www.aventuranauticamenorca.com)* provides a tour with modern high performance dinghies, including a break for snorkelling. The three-hour boat trip costs around 60 euros per person (incl. softdrinks). You'll pay less than half of that at *Menorca Nord (in the summer daily 10am and 2pm | 28 euros | C/ Gurmesind Riera 98 | mobile tel. 6 53 87 61 34 | www.menorcanord.com)*, for a small fee, they'll also pick you up from your hotel *(40 euros)*.

WATER SPORTS

Diving Center Fornells (Passeig Marítim 68 | tel. 9 71 37 64 31 | mobile 6 19 41 41 51 | www.divingfornells.com) organises interesting dives on the north coast and also offers diving lessons. Expert staff will teach you how to sail, stand-up paddleboard and windsurf at *Wind Fornells (at the harbour | mobile tel. 6 64 33 58 01 | www.windfornells.com)* afterwards, you can also hire surfboards, dinghy sailboats and catamarans. The peaceful water in the lagoon is ideal for **INSIDER TIP** trips with a kayak or stand-up paddleboard, even if you have little to no experience. You can hire both at *Katayak (Passeig Marítim 69 | mobile tel. 6 26 48 64 26 | www.katayak.net)* on the promenade.

ENTERTAINMENT

Well-heeled visitors to Menorca appreciate the evening stroll along the promenade; most tables in the restaurants are reserved in anticipation.

INSIDER TIP ISABELLA

Fornells' beach club is the ideal place for a stylish sunset cocktail: chairs in the sand, a drink in your hand, and a view of the setting sun. *C/ Tramuntana | Mobil 6 38 78 54 80 | isabella menorca.com*

BAR SA TAULA

Chill out over a cocktail and enjoy the sea view. The roof terrace provides a magical atmosphere at sunset. The design of the building (and its name) is based on the island's prehistoric landmark. *C/ Major 1*

WHERE TO STAY

CAREMA CLUB RESORT

It's not directly in Fornells, but the nearby apartment hotel *Cala Tirant* has a 2,000-m^2/21,525 sq ft waterpark *(daily 11am–5pm Uhr)*: It's warmweather fun for the whole family! *193 apartments | Urbanización Playas de Fornells | Cala Tirant | tel. 9 71 15 42 18 | www.caremahotels.com | Moderate*

⭐ **Fornells**
The charm of the old fishing port on a delightful lagoon contrasts with the otherwise rugged north coast → p. 52

⭐ **S'Albufera des Grau**
More than 90 bird species inhabit the second largest wetlands in the Balearics → p. 56

⭐ **Cap de Cavalleria**
Rugged northern cape with lighthouse and spectacular views → p. 57

⭐ **Cap de Favàritx**
Black slate coast – with a lighthouse in the middle → p. 58

⭐ **Monte Toro**
Magnificent views from the highest peak on the island – and meals in the convent restaurant → p. 60

MARCO POLO HIGHLIGHTS

HOSTAL PORT FORNELLS

The small, family-run hotel boasts a stunning view over the bay at Fornells. It has peaceful, sunny terraces, is surrounded by greenery and lies just outside the town. Rental cars and bikes are available for excursions. Free WiFi. *23 rooms | C/ des Port Fornells | Urb. Ses Salines (approx. 1 km/0.6 mile from Fornells) | tel. 9 71 37 63 73 | www.hostalportfornells. com | Moderate*

INFORMATION

OFICINA D'INFORMACIÓ TURÍSTICA
C/ Major, 57 | tel. 9 71 15 84 30 | www.aj-es mercadal.org | only in the summer

WHERE TO GO

S'ALBUFERA D'ES GRAU ★ ◉
(129 D–E 3–5) (*ΩΩ H–J 3–5*)

A salt-water lagoon separated from the sea by a narrow dam, flowering meadows and endless forest around it all: At 34.4 km2, S'Albufera des Grau is the second-largest wetland area on the Balearic Islands (the largest is on Mallorca). It is also the heart of the Unesco Biosphere Reservation. Additionally, its coastline is a protected area; the beach is natural, and often covered in seaweed. The animals love that they can live here undisturbed: Many bird species brood on the shores of the shallow water, including ospreys and herons. The salt-water lagoon is full of wriggling eels and paddling turtles.

But if this is a protected area, can you still see and experience all of these beautiful creatures and landscapes for yourself? Yes! Visitors are allowed to hike through the nature preserve: A wooden walkway leads across marshes, and marked trails wind their way uphill to vantage points. Shortly before you enter *Es Grau* (see p. 58), where you will also find dining options, there is a pavilion with information about the hiking trails. This is also the starting point for the ● free two-and-a-half-hour tours offered by the rangers (in Spanish only). Tour groups are limited

Hiking, swimming, sailing: Outdoor fun at the S'Albufera des Grau National Park

to 20 people, so make sure to register for the tour in advance by phone.

If you want to take a **INSIDER TIP** short hike on your own, follow the signs to ☲ *Mirador*, a vantage point high above the sea that you can reach within fifteen minutes (one direction). At the visitors' centre a little farther north, you can learn more about the nature in the marshlands – and about how extremely close S'Albufera des Grau came to being destroyed by construction projects. At the start of the 1970s the *Shangri-La* holiday resort was built on the eastern banks of the lagoon and it was only massive protests by the population that brought the project, already under construction, to a halt.*Centre de Recepció Rodríguez Femenias (Tue–Thu 9am–5pm, Fri–Sun 9am–3pm | admission free | Ctra. Maó–Es Grau, Me-9, km 3.5, turnoff "Llimpa" | southeast of Fornells | tel. 9 71 17 77 05)*.

CALA BINIMEL·LÀ & CALA PREGONDA (128 A2) (*⌖ F2*)

The *Cala Binimel·là* bay is accessible via a dirt road; enjoy the ambience of the shady garden at the restaurant *Binimel·là* (see p. 99). If you continue along the path to the coast, the beaches will become grittier and turn red, and the cliffs will be covered with a carpet of *socarells*. This native plant looks like soft moss from a distance, but if you inspect it more closely or even touch it, you'll discover that it's actually quite thorny.

Feel like a swim on a secluded beach? Then follow the coastal trail (in full sun) from the western end of the bay to neighbouring *Cala Pregonda*. It's about a 10-minute walk: The white sandy beach is lined with incredible rock formations that look like they were carved by a sculptor, and you can see straight through the crystal-clear water down to the bottom of the bay.

CALA TIRANT (128 B2) (*⌖ F2–3*)

Another stunning bay is cut so deep into the northern coast that it's safe to swim here. Just outside of Fornells – near the Ses Salines salt pans – the road to the bay branches off to the left. A cluster of little white holiday homes climbs up the eastern slope of the bay, whilst the western side is undeveloped. From the wide, sandy beach, you'll have a view of sloping, unspoiled cliffs.

CALA DE SA TORRETA (129 E4) (*⌖ J4*)

Looking for a secluded beach? Then park your car in the town of Es Grau, on the small bridge over the La Gola canal, and follow the marked *Camí de Cavalls* trail northward. Even before you crest the first rise, you'll see an unspoiled bay 3 km/1.9 mile ahead – it takes its name from a tower *(torreta)*. After another half hour, you'll reach the Cala de Sa Torreta.

CAP DE CAVALLERIA ★ ☲ (128 B1) (*⌖ F2*)

Even the ride to Menorca's northern cape over windswept steppes is an adventure – sometimes, you'll even met a few wild goats here. The view from around the lighthouse, which stands proudly on this northern cape, is simply stunning. To the left, over massive drops, you can see the rocky island *Illa des Porros*, to the right, the *Cap de Fornells*; towards the north, the view extends far over the sea to the horizon, towards the south to the deeply indented *Cala Tirant* bay and inland to *Monte Toro*, Menorca's highest mountain. If you're interested, you can also visit an exhibit on Menorca's five lighthouses in the former caretaker's cottage *(in the summer daily 10.30am–8.30pm | admission 3 euros | with outdoor café)*. West of the cape you can find fantastic beaches: The wild, romantic *Platja de Cavalleria* (or Ferragut), the *Cala*

Binimel·là and the *Cala Pregonda* are connected to the hiking path *Camí de Cavalls* (see also "Discovery Tours", p. 98/99).

CAP DE FAVÀRITX ★ ☼
(129 E3) (*ᗰ J3–4*)
This is where Menorca's dark side comes out, wild and rugged. The little road that branches off from the Me-7 ends after just 10 km at a black-and-white-striped lighthouse that juts out from a landscape of slate – piles of black slabs as far as the eye can see, eroded by the waves and shining silver in the surf. It's a magical place!

ES GRAU (129 E4) (*ᗰ J4–5*)
The small fishing port (32 km/20 miles southeast of Fornells and 8 km/5 miles north of Maó) is becoming a more and more popular destination for Menorcans and the narrow street and port bars are very busy, especially at weekends. Fine grey sand, a gently sloping beach, pro-tected from the wind and waves by the island of Colom, and its almost perfect semi-circular shape are the features that define Platja des Grau beach. However, in summer the bay throngs with pleasure crafts. *Menorca en Kayak (C/ S'Arribada 8 | www.menorcaenkayak.com)* offers kayak courses and excursions. Once you have done the course you can also hire boats and set off on your own. You'll find simple snacks with a beachside view at *Bar Es Grau* (see p. 101).

ILLA D'EN COLOM ● (129 E4) (*ᗰ J4*)
This little island off the eastern coast is a natural paradise with rugged shores, se-cluded bays, and two sandy beaches. It's part of the S'Albufera des Grau nature preserve, so it's protected from construc-tion and development for tourist pur-poses. In summer a pleasure boat *(depar-ture from the port in Es Grau, Moll d'es Magatzems | four times daily)* makes the 500 m/547 yds crossing and will take you to the most beautiful bays. The remains of an British quarantine hospital and a basilica are buried beneath undergrowth, waiting to be uncovered. And if you hap-pen to fall in love with the island: You can buy it for six million euros.

LOW BUDGET

The *Hostal S'Algaret (March–Oct | Plaça S'Algaret 7 | tel. 9 71 37 65 52 | www.hostal-salgaret.com),* at the port in Fornells, offers very good val-ue for money. There are 23 rooms from 45 euros and a swimming pool.

However, it has competition from the cosy, welcoming hostel *La Palma (Plaça S'Algaret 3 | tel. 9 71 37 66 34 | www.hostallapalma.com)* locat-ed nearby, which has 20 even more beautiful rooms starting from 50 eu-ros, a pool and a delicious break-fast buffet.

ES MERCADAL

(128 B3–4) (*ᗰ F4*) **This little town in the centre of the island is a popular stop on the way to Menorca's highest mountain. Enjoy a stroll through the wide streets, past the little white houses and through the markets.**
But above all the town (pop. 5400) holds culinary promise to Menorcans as many family celebrations are given pride of place in the restaurants. Es Mercadal is also well-known for the production of cakes and pastries. *Avarques*, the sleek,

Where should we go next? Stroll through the Es Mercadal evening market

beautiful sandals with rubber tyre soles and leather straps, are produced here on Menorca and are an iconic fashion item.

FOOD & DRINK

MOLÍ DES RACÓ

In spite of its simple furnishings this is a good tip for those wanting to enjoy authentic Menorcan cuisine, in a lovely, 300 year old mill with a nice, relaxed ambience. If you want to save money, take a cue from the locals and order your meals as takeaway from the kitchen – they'll make for a great beach picnic! *Daily | C/ Major 53| tel. 9 71 37 53 92 | www.restaurantemolidesraco.com | Moderate*

TAST RESTAURANTE

A wide range of tapas, a cultured ambience and an interesting mixture of traditional Menorcan and modern creative cuisine. *Plaça Pare Camps 21 | tel. 9 71 37 55 87 | www.tastmercadal.com | Moderate*

SHOPPING

Every Thursday you can meet the artisans at the *Mercat Artesanal (7pm–10pm, in winter 6.30pm–9.30pm | Plaça del Pare Camps)*. A folklore group plays music to dance to. Looking for the iconic Menorcan sandals? The **INSIDER TIP** *avarques* workshop *(Taller Gabriel Servera)* can be found in *Carrer Metges Camps 3*. The well-known confectioner *Cas Sucrer (Sa Plaça | www.cassucrer.es)* produces excellent quality *turrón* (which can be marzipan, ground peanuts, Turkish honey or chocolate) and *amargos* (almond paste). To die for!

WHERE TO STAY

JENI

This guesthouse in the town centre is more suited for a flying visit to the Es Mercadal area than a long stay. The rooms are basic but clean and there is a small swimming pool in the garden, and the food is appreciated not only by guests. *36 rooms | Mirada del Toro 81 | tel. 9 71 37 50 59 | www.hostaljeni.com | Moderate*

WHERE TO GO

MONTE TORO ★ ☽
(128 B4) *(ⓜ G4)*
Like a hedgehog with antennae and spines, the 357 m/1230 ft Monte Toro *(El Toro)* rises up out of the slightly hilly landscape. The island's highest elevation offers not only a fantastic panoramic view of Tramuntana to the north and Migjorn to the south but is also a point of orientation for the fishermen at sea, and also provides wide areas of Menorca with good radio and TV reception. At the eastern entrance of Es Mercadal an access road branches off to Monte Toro.

Today it is mainly holidaymakers who make the pilgrimage to the *Monte*, the nickname the Menorcans know the mountain by. The 17th century *Mare de Deu del Toro* chapel nestles in the shadow of the transmitter masts. It is from here that the bishop gives the island his blessing in May. The Madonna is the patron saint of Menorca. In a vault next to the chapel, Franciscan nuns sell religious souvenirs, books and postcards. The *convent restaurant Sa Posada del Toro (only during the day | tel. 9 71 37 51 74 | www.saposadadeltoro.com | Budget)* serves good Menorcan food, generous portions and an affordable lunch menu. *Sa Roca de S'Indio*, the "Indian's head" carved by nature into the rock, is rather less spectacular than its fame would suggest; it can be seen from the main Es Mercadal–Maó road on the right-hand side, immediately beyond Es Mercadal **(128 B4)** *(ⓜ F4)*.

PORT D'ADDAIA

(129 D3) *(ⓜ H3)* **The bay winds its way deep into the interior rather like a river, thus providing natural protection to one of the few harbours on Menorca's north coast.**

The slopes of the inlet are covered with evergreen bushes and the landscape seems quiet and sleepy. The unobtrusive buildings of the holiday resort are harmoniously integrated into the landscape. And the little marina on the east side of the "fjord" is also wonderfully tranquil. On the west side, you'll find the fishing harbour next to the holiday resort *Na Macaret*. But just a few kilometres further east (up to the Cap de Favàritx), the landscape paints a very different, more dramatic picture: black shale that has been shaped over millennia by the wind and sea into bizarre shapes.

FOOD & DRINK

CORNER CAFÉ BAR
English name, Mediterranean cuisine and much more than just a bar: Choose several different kinds of tapas to experience Chef Pere's distinctive style, or just order a seafood *fideuà* (paella with pasta) straight away. Enjoy the lovely ambience on the shady terrace with wicker chairs; live music on Saturday afternoons. *Daily | Av. Port d'Addaia Local 4 | tel. 6 09 00 45 21 | Moderate*

SPORTS & ACTIVITIES

DIVING & SNORKELLING
The perfect diving spot is at your doorstep: The harbour diving centre *Blue Dive*

Menorca (daily 8am–8pm | Zona Comercial Port d'Addaia | tel. 9 71 94 02 51 | blue divemenorca.com) offers a wide range of courses, from a snorkel safari (40 euros) to scuba diving. The seashore and the little islands of Addaia and Cala Macaret are protected by nature conservation laws, so they're the perfect place to spot lots of sea creatures.

WHERE TO STAY

SA TORRE BLANCA (129 D4) (*ω J4*)

The successful dairy farmer rents out his tower: fine holiday accommodation for up to three people. And you can enjoy unspoilt countryside on the edge of the S'Albufera d'Es Grau nature reserve with a view of Cap de Favàritx. *On the road to Cape (C1) signposted | tel. 9 71 18 83 08 | www.satorreblanca.com | Moderate*

WHERE TO GO

ARENAL D'EN CASTELL
(128 C2–3) (*ω H3*)

It's no wonder that a holiday resort was build on this stunning, semi-circular bay. The 500-metre-long beach is one of the island's most beautiful, surrounded by green cliffs and gently sloping into the sea, which is often crystal-clear. The *Castell Playa Fiesta (Closed Nov–April | 265 rooms | Platja d'En Castell | tel. 9 71 35 80 88 | www.palladiumhotelgroup.com | Expensive)* is a family hotel for the discerning guest. It has a sauna, swimming pool, jacuzzi and play area.

ARENAL DE SON SAURA
(128 C2) (*ω G3*)

Small holiday resort with a clean, white, semicircular sandy beach around 300 feet long. There is a simple restaurant, waterskiing, surfing and pedalo hire. If you'd like a bit more peace and quiet,

Green cliffs, crystal-clear water: Beach life at Arenal d'en Castell

then you can take the path (about 1.2k km/0.75 mile) at the left end of the beach to the next small cove, *Cala Pudent*, where there are usually only a few bathers.

SON PARC (128 C2) (*ω G3*)

The first – and currently only – golf course on the island is nestled among pine groves and the buildings of a developing holiday resort. The compact 18-hole course primarily offers long, quick-to-play, relatively easy greens; the landscape is slightly hilly and surrounded by pristine nature. The course is open all year. There is also an attached tennis court and a clubhouse with showers, a bar and a restaurant. *Urbanització Son Parc | Es Mercadal | enquiries and reservations tel. 9 71 18 88 75 | www.golfson parc.com*

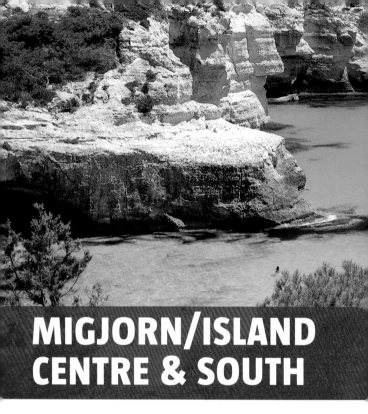

MIGJORN/ISLAND CENTRE & SOUTH

The north of the island is black, red and brown, the coast wild and rugged. Central and southern Menorca are completely different, however: The middle of the island is full of gently rolling hills covered in meadows and forests, whilst the south boasts captivating long beaches and azure bays.

Farming is important here. Much of what you'll find on your dinner plate grows in the fields between the dry stone walls: aubergines, artichokes, tomatoes. On the southern tip of the island, the ravines *(barrancs)* have cut their way into the sandy limestone at depths of up to 40 m/130 ft. Their lush greenery has earned them the name "the gardens of Menorca." There are beautiful bays with white sandy beaches where the ravines

flow into the sea, and spectacular cliffs tower above the shores.

It's no wonder that some of the island's most popular holiday destinations can be found in the south – like the white beach of Cala Galdana, the long shores of Sant Tomàs/Son Bou and the tranquil cove of Cala Trebalúger. The seawater shimmers in turquoise and azure above the white limestone – a travel ad couldn't be more beautiful! Incidentally, the climate in the south is much more comfortable than in the north, as the region is in the path of the dry, cool Tramuntana winds.

The island's native peoples were the first to recognise the benefits of the south where they primarily settled. That fact is evidenced today by the many archaeological sites – 60 per square kilometre. That

The delightful side of the island – the longest beaches, the most famous bays and the largest hotels are here on the southern coast

means Menorca has the highest density of prehistoric sites in all of Europe!

ALAIOR

(130 C3) *(🗺 G5)* **Picturesque white-washed houses stacked on the hilltop overlooked by a centrepiece church and small cobblestone streets just waiting to be explored; this is Menorca's unspoilt, authentic side away from the hordes of tourists! Alaior (pop. 9400) is the main town in the third largest municipality on the island and home to Menorca's university.**

Alaior is also regarded as synonymous with the island's famous cheese. The Coinga agriculture co-operative alone, who produces Menorcan cheese with the Queso Maó designation of origin, has a stock of over 10,000 dairy cows maintained by around 100 happy dairy farmers. Another well-known brand in the area is *La Payesa* and, until a few years ago, local milk was also used by *La*

Menorquina, an up-market brand of ice cream very popular throughout the Balearics. In addition to cows and cheese, a shoe factory is managing to hold its head above water in Alaior (pronounced: *aló*), and costume jewellery is also produced here in family businesses.

stand in stark contrast to the sea of white-washed houses around. A side entrance leads you into its dimly lit interior where the gold-leaf Baroque altar will undoubtedly catch your eye. Alaior's third church, *Sant Pere Nou,* stands on the hillside and marks the spot close by for the start of the

Alaior: once famous for its woollen goods, but now for Menorcan cheese

The town was founded in 1304 and soon made a name for itself as a prosperous producer of woollen goods. Many of the older buildings date from the flourishing 17th century including the former Franciscan monastery *Sant Diego* from 1629, a white cube with clock tower, which today houses an exhibition centre. The adjacent monastery with cloister, *Pati de Sa Lluna,* is definitely worth a visit. Local art is exhibited in the town hall built in 1612 *(ajuntament)* and located on the main road through the town. The palace building opposite houses a school of the University of the Balearic Islands. The massive Baroque church of *Santa Eulària* is just a few feet away; its brown sandstone walls

Camí del Cos horserace held every year to coincide with the town's patron saint celebrations (on the 2nd weekend in August). Menorca's prettiest cemetery *(cementiri)* is worth the few minutes' walk: monumental mausoleums sheltered by cypresses, palm trees and bougainvillea.

FOOD & DRINK

ES FESTUC

More of a traditional tapas bar than a restaurant, but the tapas are prepared with love. This locale also serves red beet hummus *(hummus de remolacha),* cheese with pesto, and wonderful desserts. *Daily 7am–midnight | C/ Es Carre-*

ro 38 | tel. 9 71 37 93 82 | www.facebook.com/esfestuc | *Budget*

FORN DE TORRE SOLI NOU
Housed in a traditional Menorcan building with a spectacular terrace. But its interior is also spot on, the meat dishes excellent and the ice cream homemade. *Urbanització Torre Soli Nou 28 | main road towards Son Bou | tel. 9 71 37 28 98 | www.esforntsn.com | Moderate*

SHOPPING

During the summer, there is an arts and crafts market (with tastings of regional specialities, folk music and workshops) in the centre on Wednesday evenings *(7–11pm)*. You can pick up classic ladies' and gentlemens' shoes at *Pons Quintana (Centre Comercial Balearica | C/ Sant Antoni 120 | www.ponsquintana.com)* and also very elegant shoes at the shoe factory *Gomila Melia S. A. (C/ Miguel de Cervantes 46 | www.gomila.es)*.
You can sample, and buy cheese at *Coniga (Ctra. Nova Parc 78 | www.coniga.com)* or at *La Payesa (Pons Martín | C/ Es Banyer 64 | www.lapayesa.es)*.

INFORMATION

Tourist info in the San Diego monastery: *Mon–Sat 10am–1.30pm, 5.30–9pm, Sun 4–9pm | tel. 9 71 37 83 22 | www.alaior.org*

WHERE TO GO

TORRALBA D'EN SALORT ★
(130 C3) *(ꕔ G5)*
This *talaiot* settlement from around 1000 BC, extended just a few years ago into an archaeological park, is situated on the secondary road from Alaior to Cala en Porter (km 3). The *Sa Taula de Torralba* shrine is a special point of inter-

est. It's an enormous t-shaped "table" in the middle of a carved stone pagan worship site – one of the best-preserved on the island. Animal bones and a small bronze figure of a bull were found near the circle of megaliths. During the full moon, INSIDER TIP night tours are available *(10 euros);* the taula is bathed in mystical illumination. *June–Oct Tue–Sat 10am–8pm, Sun/Mon 10am–1pm, Nov–May Mon–Sat 10am–1pm, 3–6pm | admission 4 euros*

TORRE D'EN GALMÉS ★ ●
(130 B3) *(ꕔ G5–6)*
You can reach one of the most extensive archaeological excavation sites on the Balearic Islands via a dirt road that branches off from the Alaior-Son Bou country road at the 2.5-km mark. Three *talaiots* and a *taula* sanctuary must have formed a small town around 1400 BC, of which the remains of rooms, defensive walls, cisterns, caves and storage chambers are still to be seen. The burial cham-

★ **Basílica de Son Bou**
Ruins on the beach with a mysterious aura – relics of a former basilica → p. 72

★ **Torralba d'en Salort**
The most beautiful and best preserved *taula* on Menorca → p. 65

★ **Torre d'en Galmés**
A complete town was created from three *talaiots* and one *taula* sanctuary → p. 65

★ **Cala Galdana**
A picturesque bay surrounded by tree-dotted cliffs → p. 68

MARCO POLO HIGHLIGHTS

ber, situated a little beyond the other remains, (today known by the name of *Ses Roques Llises*) is also outstanding, as is a hall covered with stone blocks, *Sa Camera de sa Garita*, which was probably used as a storage or assembly room. *Mon–Sat 10am–2pm, 4pm–8pm, Sun 10am–2pm | admission 4 euros, free on Mondays, free admission March–Nov, then info centre closed*

FERRERIES

(127 E4) *(ıɲ E4)* **With its rust-red cliffs, reddish brown fields and a new part of the town near the main road which is certainly not a thing of beauty, the town of Ferreries (pop. 4600), at first view, is rather off-putting.**

However, an atmospheric old town in the upper area more than compensates for those first negative impressions. Carrer de Sa Font, especially, has nooks and crannies exuding an ancient charm, and the environmental museum *Centre de Geología de Menorca (p. 108)* is also well worth seeing.

The name of the place conjures up thoughts of iron and early iron processing. However, the town did not acquire any real significance until a road linking Maó and Ciutadella was built, establishing Ferreries in the island's trading network.

FOOD & DRINK

RESTAURANTE LIORNA
An idiosyncratic mix of art and gastronomy with changing menus and exhibitions. The pizzas are recommended. If you are looking for a creative ambience and are willing to overlook serving errors, then this is the place for you. *Daily 8pm–11pm | C/ de Dalt 9 | tel. 9 71 37 39 12 | Expensive*

SHOPPING

The Mercat de Nit, a popular Friday market in the centre *(July/Aug 7–11pm)*, sells fruit, vegetables, cold meat, cheese and other island specialities as well as arts and crafts. You really must try out the *bunyols de fromatge* in one of the bakeries in the old town, dough fritters fried in oil with a cheese filling, a local speciality. The goldsmith *Núria Deyà (C/ Ciutadella 12a | tel. 9 71 37 35 23 | www.nuriadeya.com)* makes lovely jewellery with natural motifs and simple shapes in her small workshop.

CALZADOS RIA S.L.
Avarques, the typical Menorcan sandals, have been made here since 1947. They have cow leather uppers and car tyre soles. Showroom next door. *C/ Trencadors 25 | tel. 9 71 37 30 70 | www.ria.es*

INSIDER TIP ▶ HORT DE SANT PATRICI
It's hard to think of a nicer setting to learn about local cheeses and taste some too: set in Mediterranean gardens, this estate is located 1 km/0.6 mile to the north of Ferreries. While the manor house accommodates the *Ca Na Xini* hotel (see below), the former pigsties have been transformed into a cheese museum where visitors can find out how some of Spain's best dairy products are made. You also get the opportunity to taste the homemade dairy produce and wines. The delicatessen sells honey, homemade jams and smoked sausage. *Sale Mon–Sat 9am–1pm and 4–6pm, in the summer until 8pm, Sun 9am–1pm | admission 4.50 euros | Camí de Sant Patrici | tel. 9 71 37 37 02 | www.santpatrici.com*

ENTERTAINMENT

In summer you can watch demonstrations by the best Spanish riding school

Country estate, hotel, cheese museum: Hort de Sant Patrici

the *Club Escola Menorquina (June–Sept Wed and Sun from 8.30pm | Ctra. Ferreries–Cala Galdana, km 0.5 | reservations and info: tel. 9 71 37 34 97).*

WHERE TO STAY

CAMPING S'ATALAIA
S'Atalaia, one of the island's two official camp sites, is situated on the main Ferreries–Cala Galdana (km 4) road. It has good facilities, a swimming pool, clean showers and a small supermarket and is only about 3 km/2 miles from the sea. *Tel. 9 71 37 42 32 | www.campingsatalaia.com | Budget*

INSIDER TIP CA NA XINI ☺
Those who spend the night will not want to leave: set in romantic grounds, the villa's historic architecture and minimalistic design are sure to please as is the breakfast with homemade, organic specialities, served al fresco and accompanied by the sounds of birds singing. The hotel is connected to the *Hort de Sant Patrici* estate with dairy, cheese museum and bodega where you can acquaint yourself with traditional Menorcan cuisine. No children allowed! *8 rooms | Camí de Sant Patrici | tel. 9 71 37 45 12 | www.canaxini. com | Expensive*

SES SUCRERES
The sweets for the children of Ferreries were once made in this country manor house. For the last few years, it has been providing accommodation with six individually designed rooms: simple, clean and in typical Menorcan ambience. You also get free homemade sweets. *Open all year | C/ Sant Joan 15 | tel. 9 71 37 41 92, mobile 6 44 26 02 27 | www.hotelsessucreres.com | Moderate*

SON TRIAY AGROTURISMO
On the same main road as the campsite (see above, turn off to the right) you come to this country B&B with a swimming pool and a tennis court. *14 rooms | tel. 9 71 15 50 78 | www.sontriay.com | Moderate*

FERRERIES

INFORMATION

Town hall | Carrer de Sant Bartomeu 55 | tel. 9 71 37 30 03

WHERE TO GO

BINISSUES (127 E3) (*⨅ d3*)
If you are driving from Ferreries toward Ciutadella, it's recommendable to take a detour after 4 km (junction: Cami Els Alocs) to Binissues. Be a fly on the wall at the old country estate of the noble Salort family and learn how the affluent upper class once lived and how they earned their money. In the outbuildings, you can view the dairy, sausage-making workshop, bakery, and threshing floor – and also join a tasting if you want to try the home-made products. Additionally, you can get an overview of Menorca's landscapes in the little natural history museum, and at the ☆ restaurant (*Moderate*), enjoy Menorcan cuisine and a spectacular panorama view of the hilly green landscape. *May–Oct Tue–Sun 10.30am–5pm, restaurant until 11pm | admission 7 euros | tel. 9 71 37 37 28 | www. binissues.com*

CALA GALDANA ⭐ (127 D5) (*⨅ D5*)
At one time this green oasis, surrounded by dark grey coastal cliffs, was described as "picturesque" or "like paradise". Unfortunately its charm is today being buried under concrete: the *Cala Galdana* resort is constantly expanding with new apartments, holiday flats, restaurants and supermarkets, especially into the western foothills of the bay. As you arrive, level with the first hotel (turn off to the left), you will gain a ☆ good overview. The beach is a good 500 m/528 yds long with fine golden sand making it ideal for families with small children. The sea within the bay only becomes rough with

a southerly wind, which is rare. The lovely *El Mirador* (*daily | tel. 9 71 15 45 03 | www.elmirador-restaurante.com | Expensive*) restaurant has a pleasant terrace and serves a wide range of grilled meat and fish and has a fantastic location: carved into the rock on the peninsula off the coast.

The modern ☆ Hotel *Audax Spa & Wellness (244 rooms | Urbanització Serpentiona | tel. 9 71 15 46 46 | www.art-iemhotels.com | Expensive)*: is also in a fantastic location: barely 100 m from the beach, with a stunning view of the picture-postcard bay. It also boasts a spa area of more than 700 m²/7535 sq ft and free WiFi. The enormous hotel ☆ *Meliá Cala Galdana (341 rooms | tel. 9 12 76 47 47 | www.melia.com | Expensive)* might be a bit of an eyesore from the outside, but if you stay there, you'll have an incredible view of the sea, an extremely comfortable room and access to two swimming pools and an infinity pool. The INSIDER TIP *Beach Club El Cape Nao (closed Oct–April)* with its terrace over the sea is also open to non-guests.

If you are looking for unspoilt countryside on Menorca, then near Cala Galdana you will find the *Binisaid* estate *(4 rooms | Ctra. Ferreries–Cala Galdana, km 4.3 | tel. 9 71 15 50 6 3 | www.binisaid.com | Moderate)*, one of the first "alternative" holiday offers on Menorca, which enjoys an enchanting location between the *barrancs*, surrounded by forest and only a few miles from the coast, with stunning beaches nearby and a swimming pool. Enjoy homemade jam, sausage and cheese for breakfast.

Motor boats, dinghies and kayaks for the whole family are available at *Sports Nautics (on the beach | tel. 6 76 99 12 44 | May–Oct)*. Several times a week, excursion boats set sail from Cala Galdana out to sea, heading along the south coast.

One provider is *Menorca en Barco (mobile tel. 6 05 49 29 93 | www.menorcaenbarco.com)*. An alternative is the water taxi from INSIDERTIP *Menorca Taximar (May–Oct daily 9am–2pm every full hour from Cala Galdana | 25 euros per person return | www.menorcataximar.com)*. It visits half a dozen distant beaches (and grottoes), and you can decide which "playa" you'd like to spend the next few hours basking on. You will be picked up at a fixed time and ferried back to your starting point.

CALA MITJANA ● (127 D–E5) (*ꝋ D5*)
The bay is often called "Spain's Caribbean"; for some, it is one of the most beautiful bays in the whole Mediterranean. The bay can be reached by a footpath over the cliffs (roughly 1 km/0.6 mile) or by car (1.5 km/1 mile before Cala Galdana to the left). It is worth the walk, because you are rewarded with a 100 m/300 ft long beach with fine white sand followed by a pine forest. Follow the path further in an easterly direction and it leads to the lovely, quiet ● *Cala Trebalúger* (approx. an hour's walk, some of it not easy, from Cala Galdana). Unfortunately, access to the bay has been closed by the landowner; however, no one can stop you, not even the owner, from approaching from the sea side (and this also includes a 100 m wide coastal strip).

Numerous caves and sites of prehistoric finds are to be found in the course of the ravines, which later feed into Cala Trebalúger. Roughly halfway between Cala Galdana and Cala Sant Tomás you will find two more, usually deserted bays: *Cala Fustam*, a small beach with a backdrop of pine trees and a large cave at the end of the beach on the left and *Cala Escorxada*. Both can only be reached via a difficult path along the coast.

I want to touch the horsey!
Horse parade in Ferreries

ES MIGJORN GRAN

(127 F4–5) (*ꝋ E–F5*) **The name *Es Migjorn Gran* refers to "the great southern wind" – but it belongs to Menorca's smallest township, of all places. The town consists of just a few roads and a hill, surrounded by fields as far as the eye can see, bounded by crooked stone walls.** Here, you can experience Menorca as it once was: pretty and unspectacular, embedded in a charming landscape. One-storey homes cower around the church at the heart of town; its blue dome is sure to catch your eye. There are also a couple of excellent inns that make their livelihood from travellers heading toward the southern coast.

ES MIGJORN GRAN

Ocean breeze in your nose, the crashing surf in your ears: Mountain biker near Sant Tomás

FOOD & DRINK

S'ENGOLIDOR
Hearty, traditional Menorcan cuisine at reasonable prices. Try the pork ribs done the Menorcan way or the stingray with capers on the ✻ beautiful terrace with a view of the rural idyll. *Closed Mon and noon | C/ Major 3 | tel. 9 71 37 01 93 | www. sengolidor.com | Budget*

SHOPPING

In Binicudrell (1 km/0.6 mile south-west), the artist *Melisa Cabal (Binicudrell de Baix | mobile tel. 6 15 26 58 74 | www.melisaca bal.com)* runs a small gallery/workshop mainly exhibiting her own expressive work. Phone in advance to arrange a visit.

WHERE TO STAY

BINIGAUS VELL ●
This charming country hotel exudes a sense of discreet luxury. It has white fa-cades, splashes of colourful flowers and wooden tools. There is also a stunning outdoor pool and the opportunity to go riding on a horse from their own stables. The 20 comfortable rooms are, however, not exactly cheap. *Camí de Sa Mala Garba, km 0.9 | tel. 9 71 05 40 50 | www. binigausvell.es | Expensive*

INSIDER TIP ▶ S'ENGOLIDOR
If you decide to stay in the town, you can not only enjoy authentic Menorcan cui-sine at the restaurant *S'Engolidor* but also get rustic and cosy accommodation – and affordable. Pere Sales and his family will treat you as one of the family. *Closed Nov–April | 5 rooms | C/ Major 3 | tel. 9 71 37 01 93 | www.sengolidor.es | Budget*

WHERE TO GO

COVA DELS COLOMS (127 F5) (ⓜ E5)
The locals call the cave, which is only ac-cessible on foot (see Discovery Tour 2: A Trek Through Cova dels Coloms), "the

talaiots) were joined up to create a settlement which was clearly used not as a burial site, but as a dwelling.

SANT TOMÀS

(127 F5) (*∅ E5*) **Of all the resort towns on the southern coast, Sant Tomàs might be the most beautiful – here, you have access to multiple "playas" that are only separated from one another by rocky outcroppings.**

Beyond the town's namesake 530 m/1740 ft-long, fine-sand beach is a line of pine-dotted dunes protected by nature conservation laws. Rare sand lilies grow at the foot of these dunes. A promenade runs behind the trees, and a number of hotels are "hidden" behind that promenade – the hotel buildings aren't particularly tall. In the two or three rows behind that are villas ensconced in lush gardens. To the west of Sant Tomàs is *Sant Adeodat* beach, which seamlessly merges into the beach at *Binigaus.* The 1.2-km/0.75 mile-long, narrow coastal path runs along the foot of low sandstone cliffs riddled with caves. The caves provide some shade, which is probably why the beach is popular with nudists. Further to the west are the bays of *Cala Escorxada* and *Cala Fustam,* which are only accessible on foot (or by boat). On the eastern end of Sant Tomàs, you can take an attractive coastal path first to the *Platja de Atalis,* then to the dunes and wetlands of Son Bou, which connect to the long sandy beach *Platges de Son Bou.*

cathedral" because of its considerable size: 24 m/78 ft high, 11 m/36 ft deep and 16 m/52 ft wide. According to the most recent investigations, it was used in pre-Christian times as a cult site. It is an old superstition of the Menorcans that couples who enter the cave together will separate after a short time; people who meet independently of one another in the cave, however, would be united by the power of fate.

On the way from Es Migjorn Gran down to Sant Tomàs beach there are three archaeological sites. The *Talaiot de Binicudrell* has not been unearthed yet, a but restoration is planned. The prehistoric settlement of *Sant Agustí Vell* is well-known for a large stone building covered with beams which led earlier generations of archaeologists to the conclusion, now outdated, that the *taules* were only central supports for a covering beam construction. The third settlement, *Santa Mónica,* is therefore interesting because here a row of *navetas* (precursors of the

FOOD & DRINK

C'AN BERTO
Fish, paella, and even meat are grilled on hot stone here *(carne a la piedra). Daily | Edifici Migjorn | tel. 9 71 37 03 26 | Moderate*

ES BRUC

On the western edge of Sant Tomàs, you can sit directly at the seaside and enjoy delicious fish dishes and mussels. *Daily | Sant Tomás-Sant Adeodat | tel. 9 713 704 88 | Budget–Moderate*

ES PINS

This beach restaurant decked out in white is located between the pines on the eastern edge of Sant Tomàs. Menorcan cuisine and a great place to chill out.*Daily | tel. 9 713 705 41 | Budget–Moderate*

SPORTS & ACTIVITIES

The beach offers kayaks, SUP boards, and paddleboats *(www.sportskayak.es)*.

WHERE TO STAY

INSIDER TIP **LORD NELSON**

Renovated four-star hotel with garden next to a pine grove. All rooms have an ocean view, either a partial one from the front, or to the side across the pool. Director Rafael is one of the most dedicated hotel directors you'll ever encounter, and the rest of the staff follow his example. A wooden bridge leads directly from the hotel to the beach. *189 rooms | tel. 9 713 701 25 | www.hotelesglobales.com | Moderate*

LOW BUDGET

You can save some money by buying the delicious, spicy Menorcan cheese directly from the producer, such as at *Hijo de F. Quintana (Av. Des Camp Verd 47 | Parzelle 47 – Polígono La Trotxa | www.QuesoQuintana.com)* in Alaior or at *Subaida (Mon–Sat 9am–2pm and 5pm–9pm, in Aug also Sun 9am–2pm | Ctra. De Binifabini | www.subaida.com)* in Es Mercadal.

The simple country inn *La Trotxa (C/ La Industri | on the roundabout as you head towards Maó | tel. 9 713 787 39)* in Alaior serves a cheap and tasty full daily menu.

SON BOU

(130 A–B 3–4) *(F5–6)* **At 4 km/2.5 miles, the Platges de Son Bou are the longest sandy beaches on Menorca. Golden yellow sand and a gentle slope into the sea make these beaches the ideal spot for families.**

There was simply no way to prevent the construction of holiday resorts here; the location was just too perfect. The Sol Milanos Pinguïnos, two hulking ten-storey blocks, were first constructed on the beach in the 1970s. They stand in sharp contrast to the ruins of the ★ *Basílica de Son Bou*, an early Christian basilica from the 5th century on the eastern edge of the bay that wasn't discovered until 1951. Only the base of two rows of columns, the foundation walls and a baptismal font with a cloverleaf-shaped well still remain. Aerial photographs revealed a grid of roads that led from the church far into the sea – apparently, the sea level was much lower 1500 years ago.

FOOD & DRINK

Enjoy a break at the relaxing beach bar INSIDER TIP *Xiringuito Es Corb Mari (May–Oct daily from 10am | Playa de Son Bou | near the Hotel Sol Milanos Pinguïnos | tel. 717 706 434 | Budget–Moderate)*, it's most beautiful at sunset, with a mojito in your hand. The seafood dishes are also

Sandcastles? Bollards? Nope – it's the ruins of an early Christian basilica in in Son Bou

delicious, and there are often live bands playing. Excellent meals are also available at *Casa Andrés (daily | Centro Comercial Son Bou 39 | tel. 9 71 37 19 18 | Moderate)*. From outside, it doesn't look like much – in fact, it might even seem like a tourist trap! – but the generous portions of fried fish are delicious!

SPORTS & ACTIVITIES

SON BOU SCUBA

Diving school with highly dedicated management, offering courses for everyone from beginners to advanced divers, as well as regular outings for practice dives and dives to explore shipwrecks and caves. Diving equipment also available to hire. *April–Oct | Centro Comercial San Jaime | mobile tel. 6 96 62 82 65 | www.sonbouscuba.com*

WHERE TO STAY

CAMPING SON BOU

Clean campground in the pine forest close to the beach. Good sanitary facilities, green space, sports field and pool; the complex also includes a supermarket and restaurants. Two types of accommodation are available to book without your own camping equipment. *Ctra. de San Jaume, km 3.5 | tel. 9 71 37 27 27 | www.campingsonbou.com | Budget*

ROYAL SON BOU – FAMILY CLUB

Family-friendly apartment hotel. The 252 apartments are located in a typically Menorcan flat-roofed building with a relaxed atmosphere – less than 100 m/330 ft from Menorca's longest beach, and extremely comfortable. *Platja de Son Bou | Tel. 9 71 37 23 58 | www.royalsonbou.com | Moderate–Expensive*

SOL MILANOS PINGUÏNOS

Over 1,000 beds in two tall buildings, directly at the beach – this hotel is a heavyweight among the island's accommodation providers. Garden, pool, tennis courts and entertainment for children and teens, free WiFi. On the ☀ top floor, you can enjoy an INSIDER TIP incredible panorama view of the sea and the dunes. *Platja de Son Bou 10 | tel. 9 71 37 12 00 | www.melia.com | Expensive*

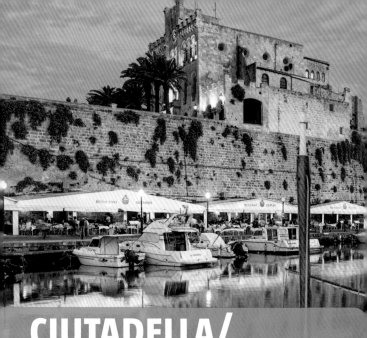

CIUTADELLA/
WESTERN TIP

Ciutadella is Menorca's most beautiful city. With its narrow alleyways and ochre-coloured houses and palaces, Ciutadella's historic district – built on a cliff over 2,000 years ago – radiates oriental charm.

It's lovely to wander through the streets and take a break on the terrace of a café under the arcades. Enjoy the relaxed atmosphere of the harbour, where the streets are absolutely lined with restaurants. The boats are tightly moored in the water, amongst them the traditional Menorcan cabin boats with their high masts.

This "small town" (as Ciutadella translates) has had many names and owners over the years: First it was called Iammo, then Iamona, then Medina Menorquina, and finally, Ciutadella. Here's a quick run-down of everyone who has controlled Ciutadella in the past: After the Carthaginians came the Romans and the Vandals, then the Arabs founded Medina Menorquina. The Aragonese eliminated any trace of the "infidels" in 1287, razing the castle and the mosque and changing the capital city's name to Ciutadella. The British denied Ciutadella the honour of remaining the capital when they took control in 1722, which Ciutadella's citizens still resent to this day.

Ancient noble families still live in Ciutadella's palaces, and the affluent have built summer villas on the edge of town. A new addition, however, are the large holiday resorts that surround it, such as Cala En Forcat in the west, mainly popular

Soft sand and ochre tones, weathered facades, cobbled streets and pastel coloured old town palaces

with the British; the luxury holiday homes resort Cala Morell in the north and the constantly expanding resorts of Cala Blanca and Son Xoriguer in the south.

CALA MORELL

(126 C2) (*m C2*) **The resorts Son Morell and Marina have merged into one holiday resort. Off season the white, uninhabited houses on the slopes of the reddish brown cliffs, eroded by the weather, at Cala Morell bay look rather incongruous.**

The architecture of the complex is reminiscent of Ibiza, with some features typical of Menorca, such as the imaginatively installed water outlets which lighten the austere appearance of many homes.

Centuries ago the original inhabitants of Menorca used a small branch of the *cala* to establish a settlement (around 900 BC) in the soft limestone caves halfway up a cliff. There are just under 20 caves, some

CALA MORELL

with support column and niches, and they are easily accessible from the road. Limestone above, rust-coloured sandstone below – this is where the imaginary line begins which geologists use to separate the much older Tramuntana, the north of the island, from Migjorn, the south of the

WHERE TO GO

CALA ALGAIARENS
(126 C2) (*ⁿ* C2)

Two quiet bays are situated within a huge private estate and they have been making headlines since 1992, because the

Ciutadella's port bay cuts deeply into the town like a fjord

island. The line runs between Cala Morell and Maó. The small, pebbly beach, however, is not necessarily worth visiting.

WHERE TO STAY

BINIATRAM
A little piece of paradise: The rustic country estate is situated about half a mile from the sea, surrounded by unspoilt nature. The property is about 500 years old and has been lovingly restored. The terraces, garden and pool also up the comfort factor. *12 rooms | Ctra. Cala Morell, km 1 | tel. 9 71 38 31 13 | www.biniatram.com | Moderate*

owner was one of the first to propose charges for access to the beach. This provoked vehement protests by the locals who had always used the area for swimming and camping – it is now a nature reserve – which led at first to the inhabitants of Ciutadella once more gaining free access, then free access for everyone. (A free parking lot is 500 m/528 yds from the beach). The beach is split in two by a rocky outcrop. The eastern section abuts a small freshwater lagoon, the remains of winter rainfall which runs off via the *La Vall* dyke and flows into the sea here.

CIUTADELLA

▨▨ **MAP INSIDE BACK COVER**
▨▨ (126 B3) (*💢 B3–4*) **Although with 29,000 inhabitants a little bigger than Maó, daily life in ★ Ciutadella is lived at a more leisurely pace than in the vibrant rival town. People seem to have more time here than in the hustle and bustle of Maó.**

Everyday life runs at a more even tempo, perhaps also a little more humane. Here the barber, when he runs out of customers in the afternoon, will warm himself a bit in the setting sun on a folding chair outside his shop. Here a stranger is often greeted with a nod of the head and the older generation here still have plenty to say, usually in a haze of thick cigar smoke and in an animated *tertulia* (discussion group) or in the shadow of the obelisk which stands like an admonishing finger over Plaça d'es Born as a reminder of the destruction of the town by a Turkish naval unit. More than 500 years have passed since that bloody attack: more than 3000 people were enslaved, the town plundered and razed to the ground so that people were forced to start again from scratch. In the 16th and 17th century the town flourished once again. Churches and monasteries were established, the centre was enclosed by town walls and it was at first home to the island diocese before finally becaming the Menorcan capital – until the occupation of the island by the British in 1722. It was only after the end of the Franco dictatorship that the island council allowed a referendum as to decide which of the two major towns should become the administrative centre of Menorca. Ciutadella was defeated by only a few votes.

SIGHTSEEING

BAIXADA CAPLLONCH (U D4) (*💢 d4*)

The *Ca'n Squella* palace and the bishop's palace *Palau Episcopal* (both 17th century) are situated on the edge of Carrer Sant Sebastia and Carrer del Bisbé. In the quiet streets the aroma of fresh bread still wafts from many a bakery in the morning. Further to the west the steps of *Baixada Capllonch* come into view leading down to the sea. The steps down to the docks are lined with souvenir stalls, boutiques and shops. To the right round the corner you come to popular *Café Balear* (see p. 81).

MARCO POLO HIGHLIGHTS

★ Ciutadella
Without doubt the most beautiful spot on the island: old and distinguished, with life lived at a leisurely pace. It is also an ideal base for exciting voyages of discovery → p. 77

★ Boat tours
Take a trip around Cap d'Artrutx to the paradise bays in the island's south → p. 83

★ Cala Macarella
White sand and turquoise water bordered by grey limestone → p. 87

★ Cala en Turqueta
A stunning bay with a gently sloping sandy beach, shady pine trees and coastal cliffs → p. 88

★ Nau des Tudons
The oldest known building in Europe → p. 88

Definitely not up to EU standards: The pots in the Museu Municipal were made a long, long ago

BASTIÓ DE SA FONT & MUSEU MUNICIPAL (U F3–4) (*f3–4*)

The original fortress from the 14th century was destroyed in 1558 by the Turks and not rebuilt until the end of the 17th century. Today, *Bastió de Sa Font* houses the *Museu Municipal*. It documents Menorca's chequered history based on historical documents, archaeological finds from the prehistoric era and the Muslim occupation, and other exhibits. *Tue–Sat 10am–2pm, May–Sept also 6pm–9pm | admission 2.46 euros (Wed free) / Plaça de Sa Font 15*

CALA D'ES DEGOLLADOR (126 B3) (*B4*)

If you're planning to spend a bit more time in Ciutadella, it's worth taking a stroll southward from the fishing and boating harbour along the fjord-like bay *(Carrer Marina/Camí de Boix)*. First, you'll pass beautiful villas, then the octagonal guard tower *Castell de Sant Nicolau (Tue–Sat 10am–1pm | free admission)*

and old fortresses that have sunk halfway into the sea. After about 500 m/547 yds, you'll reach the smaller fjord Cala d'es Degollador, which owes its gruesome name ("cutthroat bay") to a pirate raid many, many years ago. There is a tiny sand beach at the point where the bay begins to curve in the other direction, but it's more enjoyable to slip into the turquoise water from the smooth rocks.

CATEDRAL ● (U D4–5) (*d4–5*)

The Carrer Major d'es Born leads to the cathedral on Plaça de la Catedral. It owes its massive, angular appearance not least to a reinforcement of the structure after part of the dome collapsed in 1628. In 1795 a papal edict elevated the new building to the status of Cathedral of Menorca, provoking considerable criticism from Maó. The current bell tower dates back to the minaret of a mosque which dominated the square until the

13th century *(Mon–Sat 10am–4pm)*. Countless anecdotes and legends surround the church. It is said that, when the new building was constructed, the window frames had to be sealed because hundreds of birds got into the church whilst prayers were being said. In the course of history the cathedral also became a place of refuge for many people who had fallen into disfavour with the island governors of the time. Sacral treasures are on exhibition in the vestry and chapter room, including a silver rosary madonna. *Admission 3 euros, combined with the Església del Socors 5 euros | www. bisbatdemenorca.com*

ESGLÉSIA DEL ROSER (U D5) *(ω d5)*

Carrer del Roser branches off in a southerly direction from opposite the *Porta de la Llum* (light gate), the entrance to the cathedral on the right. After fifty paces you come to the narrow facade of the *Església del Roser* (1664) which is home to an interesting gallery today.

ESGLÉSIA DEL SOCORS/MUSEU DIOCESÀ (U D5–6) *(ω d5–6)*

Founded in 1648, this Augustinian monastery today houses the *Museu Diocesà*, a museum exhibiting archaeological finds, stuffed animals and paintings by local artists. The cloister and church alone are worth the visit. `INSIDER TIP` Classical concerts are held here as part of the summer festival *Festival Musica d'Estiu*. *Mon–Sat 10am–4pm | admission 3 euros | C/ Seminari 7*

MARINA (U C3–4) *(ω c3–4)*

In Ciutadella's port there is a striking difference between the right bank, used by commercial and passenger traffic, and the left bank. On the left, by the marina, there is a row of exclusive restaurants, serving well-heeled guests fresh fish.

MERCAT (MARKET HALL) ●
(U D–E6) *(ω d–e6)*

The sun only penetrates the small, quiet alleys around the market hall at around midday. But nonetheless at the *Mercat*, the market, a Mediterranean ambience characterises the scene. In the white and dark grey tiled building each guild takes up one side, the butchers looking across to the other side of Carrer de la Palma with a series of vegetable stalls and traditional market bars.

PALAU OLIVAR (U D4) *(ω d4)*

Opposite the cathedral the palace of Señor Luis de Oliver can be visited: noble halls with frescos; there's a curious frieze with all the animals on Noah's ark. Level with the palace was where formerly the *judería*, the Jewish quarter began (Carrer Palau, Carrer Sant Jeroni and Carrer Sant Francesc), with a row of simple town houses. *Mon–Sat 10am–2pm | admission 4 euros | Plaça de la Catedral 8*

PALAU SALORT (U C–D4) *(ω c–d4)*

Would you like to live here? Stroll through the many rooms of this palace; they're full of antique furniture, heavy crystal chandeliers and brocade curtains. *Mon–Sat 10am–2pm | admission 3 euros | Major d'es Born*

PLAÇA D'ES BORN (U C4) *(ω c4)*

The obelisk on Plaça d'es Born is a reminder of the *Any de sa Desgracia* (year of disaster). It casts its shadow every morning on the *town hall (Ajuntament)* which was once an Arabian fortress, then the castle of King Alfonso III – who liberated the town and island from the Moors – and later the residence of several island governors. The present building dates from the 19th century. Every year on 9 July a commemoration takes

The red-brown sandstone is a hallmark of Ciutadella: city palace at the Plaça d'es Born

place on the square recalling the event when 15,000 "infidels" laid siege to the town in 1558. It also celebrates the heroes of Ciutadella who, for seven days, bravely defied the superior forces before the town fell and was almost totally destroyed. Behind the town hall an ❋ INSIDER TIP *observation deck (Mirador)* on the town walls, the *Bastió des Governador (daily 9am–1pm),* grants magnificent panoramic views.

SES VOLTES
(U E5) (*e5*)

Ses Voltes is the name of the arcades which line *Carrer Josep M. Ouadrado* on both sides. Retail trade and small businesses thrive in the shade of the arches, each one individual and unlike any of the others. The bars on the adjoining *Plaça Nova* are usually very full, with mainly newcomers to the town enjoying a rest and a coke or lemonade. Keep go-

ing straight on and you come to *Plaça Alfons III* or *Plaça de Ses Palmeres,* as the townspeople call it, and from there to *Camí de Maó* which spans the island up to the east coast. To the west is *C/ Sant Antoni,* then *C/ Sant Josep.* Here you will find restaurants and cafés mostly frequented by locals. To the right at the end of *C/ Santa Clara* you come to the palace of the Baron of Lluriach *(Castell Lluriach),* the first nobleman of Menorca, appointed by Charles II after the battle with the Arab occupiers on Spain's south coast.

TOWN PALACES
(U C–D 4–5) (*c–d 4–5*)

In the afternoon the obelisk casts its shadow on the facades of the east side of *Plaça d'es Born.* There are a number of cafés, souvenir shops and restaurants on the lower floors of the palaces *Palau Torresaura, Palau Vivó* and *Palau Salort,*

all built in *marés*, that breathable, golden brown sandstone which was a form of building air conditioning in the past. Guided tours of the town – including the palaces – are offered by *Talaia Cultura* (mobile tel. 6 60 42 52 54 | www.talaia cultura.com).

To the north of the square is the *Cercle Artístic* – founded in 1881 and renovated at the beginning of the 1990s – and the *Teatre Municipal d'es Born*, the town theatre. In the "art circle" it is not usually art that is the topic of the day, but rather the current political issues, people sometimes being quite voluble. In the adjacent theatre, films are shown, plays performed and there is the occasional musical event. Opposite you will find the main post office, several bars and the *Sant Francesc* monastery chapel, built in 1627 on the site of an older church destroyed by pirates.

FOOD & DRINK

CAFÉ BALEAR (U E4) *(🛱 e4)*
Popular tapas and seafood stop for tourists and locals alike. The small restaurant has become an island institution with its good lunch menu and delicious seafood specialities. *Daily in the main season | Pla de Sant Joan 12 | tel. 9 71 38 00 05 | www. cafebalear.com | Moderate–Expensive*

DES PORT (U C4) *(🛱 c4)*
From this harbour restaurant in blue and white decor, you can gaze out over the harbour's fisher boats while enjoying exciting Menorcan cuisine prepared by the chef Tolo. Why not try his salad with local cheese and tomato chutney followed by sea bream with rocket or tender lamb filet on a bed of sliced potatoes? The large rock cave provides perfect shelter in bad weather. *Daily | C/ de Marina 23 | tel. 9 71 48 00 22 | Moderate*

FANG I ARAM (0) *(🛱 0)*
The only vegetarian restaurant for miles offers delightfully composed menus, also available in vegan and gluten-free versions upon request *(lunchtime Mon–Fri just 13 euros)*, breakfast on four days a week *(Mon–Thu 10.30am–noon)*. The ambience is charming and unpretentious, with a reading corner and comfy sofas. *Closes Sun | C/ Gabriel Martí i Bella 11 | tel. 9 71 38 48 71 | www.restaurantevege tarianomenorca.com | Budget–Moderate*

INSIDER TIP ▶ LA GUITARRA
(U D5) *(🛱 d5)*
In their lively cellar bar or on the terrace, Gabriel and Izaskun serve tasty and traditional Balearic cuisine such as *frito marinero* (fried seafood), *bacalao* (cod with a honey and aioli crust) and tumbet (stewed vegetables). The homemade mascarpone ice cream is the icing

A landmark in Ciutadella's old town – the restaurant Ses Voltes

on the cake. *Closed Sun | C/ Dolores 1 | tel. 9 71 38 13 55 | Moderate*

SES VOLTES (U D5) *(m d5)*

This establishment welcomes visitors from early morning to late in the night. A filling sandwich for breakfast, a snack for lunch and a fine-dining meal in the evening – this restaurant celebrates the best of what Menorcan cuisine has to offer. Housed in a three-storey old town house at the heart of Ciutadella, the restaurant serves tapas on the ground floor and à la carte menu on the first floor and on its rooftop terrace. Pintxos & cañas (diverse snacks on a stick and beer) are available on **INSIDER TIP** Wednesday evenings (from 8pm) for a token price! Friday is wine-tasting evening with a selection of local Menorcan wines to try. *C/ Ses Voltes 16–22 | tel. 9 71 38 14 98 | www. recibaria.com | Budget–Expensive*

SHOPPING

INSIDER TIP GRANEL
(U D5) *(m d5)*

Ciutadella's most appealing delicatessen selling a wide assortment of island specialities such as cheeses, smoked sausages, ham, sweet pastries, jams, honey, liquors, wine, gin, dried herbs etc. Feel free to try everything before you buy. *Ses Voltes 8 | www.granel.cat*

JAP – ARTÍCULOS TÍPICOS
(U D4) *(m d4)*

Typical Menorcan souvenirs, especially leather goods, in a little shop near the port. *Baixada Capllonch 12*

PACHAMAMA
(U C4–5) *(m c4–5)*

Affordable accessories: handmade costume jewellery and paste gems. *Plaça d'es Born 27–28*

EL PALADAR (0) (*m 0*)

Select Menorcan delicacies, in both food and beverage form: sausage and pate, ham and cheese, Menorcan honey, wine and herbal liqueur. This delicatessen only offers products produced on the island. Sample the products as part of a light lunch, then take some home with you as well! *C/ de la Creu 1 | and C/ Maó 10 | www.elpaladar.es*

PATRICIA (0) (*m 0*)

You can buy all sorts of beautiful leather goods, with the emphasis on clothes, belts, bags and shoes, not only here in the shop *(Josep Cavaller i Piris 5)*, but also (sometimes more cheaply) from the factory on the main road south *(Ctra. de Santandría). www.patricia.es*

SPORTS & ACTIVITIES

BOAT TOURS ★

Boat trips with *Rutas Marítimas de la Cruz* take you to remote beaches and bathing bays which often are otherwise not accessible. The little boat travels along sections of the western and southern coast, past *Cala de Son Saura, Cala en Turqueta* and *Cala Macarella* to *Cala Galdana.* It stops for swim breaks twice at attractive bays, and you can enjoy paella with sangria or lemonade on board the boat. The journey starts at the old harbour in Ciutadella *(June–Sept daily 9.45am);* you should arrive at the harbour by 9.30 am to secure your spot. The return trip starts at 5pm. *Ticket presale at the harbour box office, online 43 euros | Port Antic, Pantalán 1 | tel. 9 71 48 14 12 | rutasma ritimasdelacruz.com*

DIVING (0) (*m 0*)

The western tip of Menorca provides a rich and varied marine life and a wide range of diving centres. One well-established

PADI diving centre (Cala en Busqutes 10 | Edificio Las Terrazas | tel. 6 96 90 31 60 | www.scubaplus.org) is right next to the exit to Ciutadella port. It offers training, equipment hire and diving.

TENNIS (0) (*m 0*)

Public tennis court with floodlights: *Club de Tenis Ciutadella (Torre del Ram | tel. 9 71 38 84 56 | www.clubtenisciutadella.com)*

ENTERTAINMENT

Ciutadella is the hotspot on Menorca's nightlife scene and the city especially

LOW BUDGET

You can use the free WiFi in the town library. *Biblioteca Pública de Ciutadella (Casa de Cultura | Hospital de Santa Magdalena 1 | in summer Mon–Fri 9.30am–1.30pm and 6pm–8pm, in winter Mon–Fri 10am–1pm and 4pm–8pm)*

If you want to save fuel and go by bike, you can hire one at *Velos Joan* in *Ciutadella (C/ Sant Isidre 32–34 | tel. 9 71 38 15 76 | www.velosjoan. com)* or *Maó (Av. Francesc Femenias 58 | tel. 9 71 36 99 79).* They have very reasonable weekly rates.

A unique offer: buy a fish on the market in Ciutadella and let the chef in *Ulises (closed Sun | Plaça Mercat | tel. 9 71 38 00 31)* fry it for you for a modest price (2–4 euros depending on the size) where you can then eat it. The breakfast and daily specials are also reasonable and there is sheltered seating under the market's arcades.

comes to life on Saturdays. Flyers are handed out during the week advertising free entry (usually for women only) or a free drink. The locals like to start a night out on Menorca with a hearty *pa amb oli* (bread with tomatoes, garlic and olive oil), e.g. in the INSIDERTIP *Ses Persianas (Plaça d'Artrutx 2)* or in the *Sa Barreta (C/ José María Quadrado 22)*. Then they look in at the beautifully renovated and very popular *Imperi (Plaça d'es Born 7)* – to see and be seen. Here. you eat a hearty *llonguet*, a filled Menorca roll.

The late-night bars in the port area of *Es Pla de Sant Joan* are very fashionable. Where just a few years ago fishermen hauled their *llauts* ashore to repaint them in the shade of the boat houses, today there are pale flashing neon lights. This is where some of the best dance clubs are to be found: *Jazzbah (Es Pla 3)*, now a landmark on the city's club scene, still attracts large crowds. Top forty hits are played downstairs while upstairs on the rooftop terrace you can chill out with a cocktail or glass of beer. *Kopas (Sat 11.30pm–5.30am | www.kopasclub.com)*, like *Jazzbah*, frequently organises live events. Guests can dance and chill out on the various floors while the rooftop terrace offers panoramic views over the entertainment district of Es Pla.

If you're looking for something more low-key, and a cool drink accompanied by the sea's breeze sounds appealing, head for one of the many street bars. If you're looking for a no-fuss atmosphere, you should also visit *Ones (www.pubmusicalones. com)* and the ● legendary jazz bar *Sa Clau (C/ Marina 93 | www.saclau.com)*, where they mix excellent cocktails, either on the terrace or in a natural cave. Live bands sometimes fire up the crowds. Another cheek-by-jowl location in the evening is Ses Voltes and the streets around. Here you can find quieter bars

and pubs such as *La Moncloa* at the Plaça Nova and *Can Colás* at Carrer Alaior. One of the largest discos in the west of the island is *Anchors (in the Son Oleo district)*, a stylish club with spectacular lighting effects, a mixture of music and guests as well as live acts in summer. If you're still not ready to turn in for the night, follow the groups of fishermen starting their day in the INSIDERTIP *Triton (down at the jetty)*.

WHERE TO STAY

CIUTADELLA (U E6) (*m e6*)

A basic Hostal Residencia right in the centre, many rooms with en-suite bathroom and the in-house restaurant serves good regional cuisine. *17 rooms | C/ Sant Eloi 10 | tel. 9 71 38 34 62 | all year | Budget–Moderate*

HOSTAL OASIS (U C6) (*m c6*)

This Bed & Breakfast in the old town was named after the romantic garden in its courtyard. It is the most affordable accommodation far and wide with friendly, practical rooms (double room with shared bathroom 29 euros, and 35 euros with a private bathroom). Señor Nuno makes your stay truly pleasurable. *12 rooms | C/ Sant Isidre 33 | mobile tel. 6 30 01 80 08 | www.hostaloasismenor ca.es | Budget*

INSIDERTIP PORT CIUTADELLA (O) (*m O*)

This well-maintained four-star hotel in a prime location has its own bathing access to the sea (no beach!) and is located on the Cala des Degollador. It has an indoor and outdoor pool, jacuzzi, steam bath, sauna and a small beauty centre with upmarket treatments. Many rooms have balconies and a view over the bay; relaxed atmosphere thanks to the friendly, helpful staff. Free WiFi. *94 rooms and suites | Passeig Marítim 36 | tel. 9 71 48 25 20 | www.sethotels.com/es/port-ciutadella-hotel.html | Expensive*

RIFUGIO AZUL (U E4) *(Ⓜ e4)*

Located in the old part of the city, the "Blue Refuge" has a friendly and enthu-siastic owner, Mattia, who makes you feel immediately at home. Modern, wel-coming rooms (free WiFi, air condition-ing) and a suite with terrace and Jacuz-zi. Excellent breakfast with home-made cake. *4 rooms | C/ ses Andrones 33 | mobile tel. 6 34 22 68 23 | www.rifugioazul. com | Moderate*

TRES SANTS (U E5) *(Ⓜ e5)*

This charming little hotel is located in the heart of the historic district, just 100 m from the cathedral. All 8 rooms are tastefully decorated, each in its own in-dividual style. The friendly atmosphere, pool and rooftop terrace also contrib-ute to the comfort factor. *8 rooms | C/ Sant Sebastiá 2/Ecke San Cristófol | Tel. 9 71 48 22 08 | Moderate*

971 (U E5) *(Ⓜ e5)*

In a top central old town location nes-tled between the harbour and cathe-dral, this small Italian-run hotel was inspired by Italo Calvino's novel "In-visible Cities": contemporarily fur-nished rooms in a historic palace with a touch of eccentricity. *6 rooms, 1 apart-ment | C/ Sant Sebastiá 10 | mobile tel. 6 48 19 69 73 | www.971menorca.com | Moderate*

INFORMATION

OFICINA DE INFORMACIÓN TURÍSTICA (U C4) *(Ⓜ c4)*
Plaça d'es Born 15 | tel. 9 71 48 41 55 | www.menorca.es

There is always plenty going on in Ciutadella

BUSES

The intercity bus station *(TMSA bus com-pany | tel. 9 71 36 04 75 | www.tmsa.es)* is located to the south of the old town at the Plaça de la Pau (0) *(Ⓜ 0)*. The termi-nal for inner-city buses travelling to des-tinations in and around Ciutadella is in the old town at the Plaça de s'Explanada/Plaça des Pins (U B4–5) *(Ⓜ b4–5) (Torres bus company | tel. 9 02 07 50 66 | www. bustorresmenorca.com)*. Be warned: the frequency of buses depends on the time of year!

WHERE TO GO

CALA BLANCA
(126 B4) *(Ⓜ B4)*

The name refers both to the holiday resort (approx. 4 km/2.5 miles south of Ciutadella) – with no particular features to distinguish it from comparable resorts on the island – and to the bay situated on the southern edge of the resort. It owes its name (white bay) to the brilliant white sand framed by the green backdrop of a pine forest of trees. To the left and right of the beach are the coastal cliffs covered with restaurants and bars, which are better for their outstanding location rather than for remarkable food. The ☀ view of a romantic sunset is pretty much guaranteed here on most evenings, for example at the beach bar *Hola Ola (Av. Llevant 11)*. For children there is a water slide in the resort and *Cova de Parella*, well-known for its stalactites and stalagmites and a subterranean lake, is situated not far from the bay.

On the main road to Cap d'Artrutx, just before Cala Blanca, is *Es Caliu (tel. 9 71 38 01 65 | Budget–Moderate)*, a mix of beach club and drive-in, with swimming pool, barbecue specialities in the evening and still reasonable prices. Although it gets overcrowded in summer, the large restaurant *Cala Blanca*

(daily | Av. Llevant 1 | tel. 9 71 38 27 01 | www.restaurantecalablanca.com | Moderate) is famous for its speciality Paella and its seaside setting offers a nice sea breeze and the perfect place to watch the evening sunset. Another waterfront restaurant, *Miramar (daily | Av. Cala Blanca | tel. 9 71 38 62 62 | Moderate)*, serves fish and meat grilled on a hot stone.

CALA EN BOSC
(126 B5) (*M B5*)

From the Cap d'Artrutx resort you come to Cala en Bosc, the next holiday paradise. Here too the architecture of the resort is no more than average, based more on functionality than aesthetics, but the beach on the edge of the resort with fine white sand and usually clean sea water speaks for itself. Informal *chiringuitos* (beach bars) cater to every taste. The area between Cap d'Artrutx and Son Xoriguer is where the *minitren* runs, a small tourist train on rubber wheels. The established water sports school *Surf & Sail (on Son*

Pretty, prettier, prettiest: The picture-perfect bay of Cala Macarella is calling your name!

Xoriguer beach | mobile tel. 6 29 74 99 44) offers windsurfing and sailing courses in summer.

CALA EN FORCAT
(126 A–B3) (*ℳ A3–4*)

A holiday village on the coastal cliff to the west of Ciutadella. The resorts of *Cala en Blanes, Cala en Forcat* and *Cala en Brut* have become so enmeshed with the resort of *Los Delfines* that it is hard to see where one resort ends and another begins. The coastline is occupied by a number of villas with stunning sea views. Each of the bays has at least one small beach. The largest is the one at *Cala en Blanes,* around 50 m/165 ft wide. However, you will look here in vain for wide, empty beaches – at least in summer. On the western edge of *Cala en Forcat* there are some striking sea water geysers. These *bufadors* are, however, not the result of volcanic activities, but of a system of caves and ducts reacting to the water pressure. The *Globales Club Almirante Farragut (closed Nov–April | 472 rooms | tel. 9 71 38 80 00 | www.ho telalmirantefarragut.com | Moderate–Expensive)* is a tasteful four-star hotel at the finer end of mid-range.

CALA MACARELLA ★
(127 D5) (*ℳ D5*)

This is Menorca's version of paradise: clear turquoise water, bordered by a ring of grey limestone, in the background the strip of sand and a small wetland where turtles once lived. The access road is long and stony and there is a 5 euros charge of per car, ● which you can save if you park before the entrance and then walk. Sometimes, unfortunately, the beach is not as clean as it should be; quite often there is flotsam on the shore and picnic waste in the wood. At the moment, only a bar hidden in the pines caters for beachgoer's needs with simple (and overpriced) dishes. In the cliffs along the shore there are some prehistoric caves. There is a footpath branching off to the west to *Cala Macarelleta*, a nudist retreat. The best way to experience this idyllic bay is **INSIDER TIP** on the water, try a *boat tour from Ciutadella* (see p. 83).

CALA PAREJALS
(126 B5) (*ℳ B5*)

This is a place especially popular with weekend anglers from Ciutadella who come here to fish, and divers who like to explore the rich and varied underwater world. Access is via a coastal path from *Platja de Son Xoriguer.*

CALA SANTANDRIA
(126 B4) (*ℳ B4*)

This is a pioneering centre of the tourist industry which is still relatively new on Menorca. Lots of bare rock, lots of buildings, hotels, bars, villas, restaurants – and not much greenery. The beach is white and rather gritty. The entrance to the bay is guarded by an old 18th century British defence tower. What is especially interesting is the cave which Nicolau Cabrisas, the sculptor and local celebrity, used as a home and workshop. Over the years the freelance artist covered his home and workshop with masks, grotesque faces and figurines. Unfortunately, since his death, visiting the cave is no longer possible. However, the artist has also designed the adjacent restaurant **INSIDER TIP** *Sa Nacra (Cala Santandria, on the northern shore of the bay | tel. 9 71 38 62 06 | Budget–Moderate)* built directly into the cliff, with stunning romantic sunsets, candle-lit dinners, great tapas and local wines. At lunchtime there is really delicious paella. But beware: in high season you will not get in without a reservation. The *Bahía (15 rooms | C/ dels Suissos 3 | tel. 9 71 38 26 44 | www.bahia-poseidon.de/ en | Moderate)* is a small, friendly family hotel with the additional advantage that it is right next to the beach and the Poseidon diving school. At *Pedro's (C/ d'en Clates)* nightclub from May to September there is a firework display every night with laser shows and karaoke, flamenco and foam parties.

CALA DE SON SAURA
(126 C5) (*∅ C5*)

This bay is ideal for a day on the beach. It is sheltered from the wind and has two beaches, separated by a small spit of land, with fine white sand and pine trees. But beware: there are sometimes strong currents around the bay. To get here from Ciutadella you take Camí de Sant Joan de Missa at the white church of the same name and turn off right at *Son Vivó* going past the old square *Torre Saura Vell* tower. Road access to the beach is subject to a charge. The people of Ciutadella have developed a fondness for Son Saura. If the long beach is already full, a trek eastwards is worthwhile. After crossing the rocky outcrop of *Punta d'es Governador* (approx. 500 m/0.3 miles) you come to the next, considerably smaller bay, *Cala d'es Talaier*. The sand is ochre coloured and there is also a pine forest that provides shelter from the sun.

CALA EN TURQUETA ★
(126 C5) (*∅ C5*)

Along with Cala Macarella this has become the epitome of the stunning bays in the south of Menorca. Access from Ciutadella is via Camí de Sant Joan de Missa, bearing left at the fork at Son Vivó. After around 5 km/3 miles the road forks: left takes you to Cala Macarella, right to

Cala En Turqueta. The car parks are often full at weekends.

NAU DES TUDONS ★
(126 C3) (*∅ C3*)

The island's most well-known prehistoric grave and probably the oldest known building in Europe. The mighty sandstone blocks were assembled approx. 3400 years ago. In the course of the excavation the team found pieces of jewellery and the remains of human bones, suggesting that this was a plundered burial chamber.

The interior of the *nau* (Spanish *naveta*) is divided in two floors. There is a legend attached to the structure: two giants are said to have argued about a lady. As proof of their love, one was to build a two-storey tower, the other to dig a well until he found water, the first to finish won the lady's hand. The water flowed first and that so enraged the other giant that he broke a huge stone from his tower (the current entrance hole) and threw it at the giant who had dug the well, killing him. The villain then drowned himself in the well and the lady died of a broken heart. The well is still known by the name *Pou de Sa Barrina* today. *Admission 2 euros | Ctra. Me-1 between Ciutadella and Ferreries, km 40*

PUNTA NATI ● ☙
(126 B2) (*∅ B2*)

Some sheep come here looking for the herbs that sprout between the craggy rocks. In spring the inhabitants of Ciutadella also put up with the bumpy access road to Punta Nati *(Av. Francesc B. Moll)*. You'll have to travel the last few kilometres to the cape on foot, but it's absolutely worth it. The cape has been crowned by a lighthouse since 1913, from which you have a fantastic view of the sea, the rugged coastline and two bays in the east, *Cala es Pous* and *Cala es Morts* (bay of the dead). This name is based on the incident which occurred in the winter of 1910 when a French passenger ship steered into the cliffs and sank. Of the 150 people on board, only one young

taula. The age of the site is still unknown; all that is certain is that it was inhabited until the end of the Roman occupation. *Admission 3 euros | access via the path to the Platja de Son Saura*

Take the plunge from a yacht into the Cala en Turqueta

Frenchman survived the accident. Today a cross still marks the incident.

SON CATLAR
(126 C4) (*ɷ C4*)

Before you reach the tower *Torre Saura Vell* on the way from Ciutadella to here, you will see to your left the largest prehistoric settlement area in the whole Balearics, spread over 15 acres and surrounded in part by a partly ruined wall. Here you will find cisterns, the foundations of living areas, five stone towers *(talaiots)* and the central shrine, the

TORRE LLAFUDA
(127 D3) (*ɷ C3–4*)

This large prehistoric settlement – which is today losing the fight to a steadily encroaching grove of holly oaks – has a magical, almost eerie feel to it. There are rooms, chambers, artificial caves, cisterns, a stone tower and a INSIDER TIP *taula*, all in the shade of the trees. *Access via the main Ciutadella–Maó road, km 37, then right after about 250 m/273 yds*

DISCOVERY TOURS

① MENORCA AT A GLANCE

START: ① Binibèquer Vell
END: ⑬ Cap d'Artrutx

2 days
Driving time
(without stops)
3 ½ hours

Distance:
➡ 140 km/87 miles

COSTS: approx. 180 euros (including rental car, petrol, food for two adults, overnight stay in affordable hotel, e.g. **S'Engolidor** →
p. 70 in Es Migjorn Gran)
WHAT TO PACK: Swimwear, sun protection and picnic, if you'd like

IMPORTANT TIPS: If you can, start your tour on a Wednesday to coincide with the market held in ⑦ **Alaior**.
Day 2 shouldn't be a Monday, since the lighthouse restaurant **Es Far d'Artrutx** is closed on Mondays.

Would you like to explore the places that are unique to this island? Then the Discovery Tours are just the thing for you – they include terrific tips for stops worth making, breathtaking places to visit, selected restaurants and fun activities. It's even easier with the Touring App: download the tour with map and route to your smartphone using the QR Code on pages 2/3 or from the website address in the footer below – and you'll never get lost again even when you're offline.

TOURING APP

→ p. 2/3

Menorca's network of roads resembles a fish's skeleton: the island is bisected by the main vertebral spine, the Me-1 motorway, running between Maó in the east and Ciutadella in the west, with smaller roads branching off to the coast in the north and south. This tour takes you from east to west and then from north to south, to the island's former and present day capital, to lively harbours and dormant villages, to paradise bays and rugged capes – explore the island's diversity on this unique tour.

The starting point is ❶ **Binibèquer Vell** → p. 50 with a Mediterranean breakfast of croissants and a steaming cup of *café amb llet* (milky coffee) at the **Club Náutico**. The pic-

DAY 1
❶ Binibèquer Vell

Menorca

Cap de Cavalleria

5 km
3.1 mi

Cala Morell   Binimel·là   Cova Polida

Fornells

Port d'Addaia

Ciutadella   Es   Mercadal
⑫ ∴ ⑪ Me 1 Ferreries   ⑤

Naveta d'Es   ⑨
Tudons   Cala   Es Migjorn   ⑥
Cala   Sta. Galdana   ⑩ Gran S. Cristóbal
Blanca   Es Grau

⑬
Tamarinda   Cala   Alaior   Cala Mesquida
Cap   Turqueta   Sant Tomàs   Torre   ⑦ Talati
d'Artrutx   Son Bou de Baix d'en Gaumes de d'Alt ∴
                                                                ② **Maó**
                          Cala En Porter ⌂   Sant   (Mahón)
                      Cova d'En Xoroi   Climent ✈ ✈ Sant Lluís
                                                            S' Algar
           Mar Mediterrània   Binibequer Vell ①

                                                    Punta Prima

11.5 km/7 mi

② Maó

17 km/10.5 mi

③ Cap de Favàritx

25 km/15.5 mi

④ Fornells

9 km/5.6 mi

⑤ Es Mercadal

ture-perfect resort in the south-east of Menorca is a rep-
lica of a traditional pirate's cove. **From here it is about a
20 minute drive to** ② **Maó → p. 36** where you can take
in a first glance of the city by walking from the Plaça de
s'Esplanada (with car park and tourist information) to the
old town and from there down to the harbour. **To leave the
city, head along the quieter Ronda de Sant Joan, which
from the left joins the Me-7 main road to Fornells.** From
here the landscape becomes gentler, greener and more
tranquil and you will soon be driving through the island's
nature reserves in the north east.

**About halfway along the route, a country road (Cf-1) on
your right leads to the lighthouse at** ③ **Cap de Favàritx
→ p. 58**, which stands on weathered cliffs above the
sea, representing the remote, rugged face of the island. B**ack
on the Me-7** carry on to the small coastal resort of
④ **Fornells → p. 52**. Perched on the banks of the great
salt water lagoon, with fishing boats reflected in the
tranquil waters, you can enjoy a cool drink at the **Bar La
Palma** before leaving. Don't be tempted to a snack because your lunch time destination is not far away. **Head
south on the Me-15 to** ⑤ **Es Mercadal → p. 58**, popular for its restaurants serving tasty, local food. After your
meal the tour continues south, leaving the steppe land-

scape of the north coast behind to embrace pine groves which then in turn give way to the lush green pastures in the centre of the island. **On the eastern outskirts of this small town, a narrow tarmac road leads up to the barren ⑥ Monte Toro → p. 60.** After a few hairpin bends you reach a height of 357 m/1171 ft. From the "roof of Menorca" you can enjoy a fantastic panoramic view. Although you've just finished lunch in Es Mercadal, try to squeeze in a pastry and coffee in the delightful monastery restaurant Sa Posada del Toro. **En route to Maó a detour then leads you to ⑦ Alaior → p. 63,** a traditional resort famous for its arts and crafts and cheese dairies. The village market held on Wednesdays (from 7pm onwards) is a good opportunity to check out local crafts and buy some of the delicious specialities. **Back on the road to Ciutadella, the Me-16 turns off to the right after about 3 km/2.2 miles to the sleepy resort of⑧ Es Migjorn Gran → p. 69.** After a splendid meal at the delightful guesthouse S'Engolidor you can also spend the night here.

Enjoy a full breakfast **before continuing along the Me-20 and later along hairpin bends cut into the reddish brown rock cliffs to Cala Galdana.** Schedule a break at ⑨ Ferreries → p. 66 to take in the charm of the old part of town perched on the hill. **Then about 300 m/985 ft after leaving the resort, turn left onto the smaller Me-22 road.** After just under 5 km/3 miles you will be treated to a wonderful view of white sandy beaches and turquoise sea of ⑩ Cala Galdana → p. 68. Take a refreshing plunge into the waves before enjoying lunch at the restaurant El Mirador → p. 68.

Back on the Me-1, drive westwards and just before you reach the outskirts of Ciutadella, follow the road signposted on your left to one of the oldest buildings in Europe. Do not miss out on a visit to the ⑪ Nau des Tudons → p. 88: wander between the gigantic stones which appear to have been erected by giants. Now drive on to ⑫ Ciutadella → p. 77, the largest city in the west of the island and regarded by some as Spain's most beautiful. **Park near the Plaça de ses Palmeras (Alfonso III)** where you can start to explore this vibrant town (some say it's one of the most beautiful towns in all of Spain!) **by strolling along the Carrer de Maó and Carrer de Josep Maria Quadrado and then down to Plaça d'es Born.**

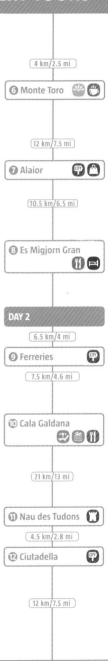

4 km/2.5 mi

⑥ Monte Toro

12 km/7.5 mi

⑦ Alaior

10.5 km/6.5 mi

⑧ Es Migjorn Gran

DAY 2

6.5 km/4 mi

⑨ Ferreries

7.5 km/4.6 mi

⑩ Cala Galdana

21 km/13 mi

⑪ Nau des Tudons

4.5 km/2.8 mi

⑫ Ciutadella

12 km/7.5 mi

⓮ Cap d'Artrutx

Then drive south along the Me-24 until you reach the spectacularly wild and rugged **⓮ Cap d'Artrutx** with its lighthouse. How about a dip in the sea at the beautiful tiny beach of **Cala en Bosc** before joining in the evening ritual on the cape? The **INSIDER TIP** terrace of the lighthouse restaurant **Es Far d'Artrutx** *(Closed Mon | Passeig Martítim | tel. 6 54 39 73 00 | Moderate)* is a great spot for watching the sunset: The rays of light transform the sea into vivid colours of yellow to saffron red. When the sun finally disappears, the spectacle is accompanied with a rapturous round of applause...

2

DARK CAVES, TURQUOISE SEA: A TREK THROUGH COVA DELS COLOMS

| START: ❶ Es Migjorn Gran | ½ day |
| END: ❶ Es Migjorn Gran | Walking time (without stops) 3 hours |

| Distance: | easy |
| 🕐 12.5 km/7.8 mi | .ıl Height: 140 m/459 ft |

COSTS: Approx. 20 euros for food
WHAT TO PACK: Protective footwear with good tread, snacks, drinking water, swimwear; torch or headlamp to explore the caves

IMPORTANT TIPS: Buses run only in summer from Ferreries and Maó to Es Migjorn Gran.

One of the island's most beautiful walks through a gorge lined with holm oaks and pine trees to a stunning beach at the end. En route you will pass a cave which resembles a bizarre "cathedral" because of its stalactites. The route returns along a picturesque path slightly off the beaten track.

❶ Es Migjorn Gran

09:00am In **❶ Es Migjorn Gran** → p. 69, treat yourself to a breakfast in the tapas bar **INSIDER TIP La Palmera** *(daily from 7am | C/ Major 83)*. **Then drive through the resort heading south-west towards the free car park near the cemetery. Take the town's main road and turn left just before you leave the town into Camí de Sa Malagraba.** After leaving your car at the cemetery, **walk along the Camí de Binigaus Nou heading south.** To the right after 500 m/1640 ft the Binigaus Vell estate → p. 70 will come into view where the road trails off into a path behind the building. **Follow the path on your**

1.5 km/0.9 mi

Gate to the underworld: Cova dels Coloms

left signposted "Cova dels Coloms". **Continue along the footpath through fields and down into the limestone gorge, the** ❷ **Barranc de Binigaus.** The landscape changes abruptly and the eroded limestone gorge fills with greenery. Aleppo pines, olive trees and holly oaks tower upwards with great northern divers and hoopoes fluttering in their branches.

Roughly halfway down to the sea, ignore the first left turn-off and, where the path forks after a short time, take the path straight on. You will soon come to the wide open mouth of the ❸ **Cova dels Coloms** → p. 70 (doves' cave). The freely accessible cave owes its name to the hunting customs of previous generations. They stretched nets across the cave entrance to catch the doves nesting inside. In the thick layer of clay on the cave floor cult objects from Menorcan prehistory have also been found, suggesting that the wide hall was once used for ritual activities. Take a break to take in the vast size of the

❷ Barranc de Binigaus

250 m/820 ft

❸ Cova dels Coloms

600 m/1969 ft

chamber towering 25 m/82 ft high and up to 110 m/360 ft long. **Return to the main path at the bottom of the gorge and follow for a short distance. After five minutes you will reach a plateau where you take a path behind a gap in the wall heading left to the barranco. Turn left after 20 m/80 ft and then right up** to the entrance of the ④ **Cova de na Polida** where you are unfortunately not allowed to enter to see the splendid stalactites due to the rare breed of bat which now resides inside. Once the ban is lifted again, you can admire beautiful stalagmites and stalagtites in the cave. **Having returned to the footpath, take the route down to the sea. When you reach a watering trough, take the signposted GR-223 path** where the gorge opens out into the ⑤ **Platja de Binigaus** beach with its fine sands and turquoise sea, perfect for a spot of bathing.

12:00pm If you have forgotten to pack a picnic, you will find something to eat at ⑥ **Urbanització Sant Tomàs To get there, follow the beach eastwards** to the beachside restaurant **Es Bruc →** p. 72. **To return to your car, walk to the end of the Platja de Binigaus and back along the same path to the watering trough. Then wander through the gorge until you reach the fork in the path after 10 minutes. Keep left and follow the cobblestone path** uphill past wild fruit trees and through wild, romantic scenery. **The path becomes wider, leading up to the Binigaus plain and back to the car park in** ① **Es Migjorn Gran**.

④ Cova de na Polida

2 km/1.25 mi

⑤ Platja de Binigaus

1 km/0.6 mi

⑥ Urbanització Sant Tomàs

7 km/4.3 mi

① Es Migjorn Gran

3 CYCLING ALONG THE NORTH COAST

START: ① Ferreries	1 day
END: ① Ferreries	Walking time 3 hours (10 km/6 mi), cycling time 3½ hours (40 km/25 mi)
Distance: very easy	
🚲 50 km/31 mi Height: 100 m/328 ft	

COSTS: Approx. 15 euros for a trekking or mountain bike, 4.50 euros for entrance to the cheese museum, food in Es Mercadel 15–20 euros
WHAT TO PACK: swimwear, headwear, plenty of drinking water, comfortable shoes, picnic and bike lock (from the bike rental)

IMPORTANT TIPS: The first section of the bike route is extremely steep – you may have to push your bike for a few minutes.
The GR-223 hiking path is marked red.

Green hills and traditional villages, rugged coasts and picturesque bays: explore the island's highlights in the north on this combined trekking and cycling tour. The cycling tour takes you along tracks and tarmac roads, making it suitable for unexperienced cyclists as is the glorious clifftop walk with many nice views along a signposted path.

08:00am This route starts at the eastern outskirts of
① Ferreries → p. 66, to be precise at the petrol station in Polígono Industrial where you take the side road Camí de Sant Patrici heading north. A signpost points to the
② Hort de Sant Patrici → p. 66, where it's worth taking your first break: This historic estate is not only surrounded by beautiful gardens, it also houses an attractive **cheese**

① Ferreries

1.5 km/1 mi

② Hort de Sant Patrici

Holiday fun: Cycling and hiking in the sunshine

museum. Take a break here for a hearty snack because you'll soon have to pedal hard: **after the next fork in the road, keep right and cycle uphill (**19 percent gradient) – don't be disheartened, even the most conditioned bikers have to get off and push at this stage. Don't give up though because the hard work will be rewarded with fantastic 360° views at the **Son Pere Nou estate** with the fjord-like Fornells bay to the north, pine tree coasts to the south, the lagoon of S'Albufera des Grau to the east and green hills all around.

Before long the tarmac path ends **and takes a sharp left to the farmhouse of Sant Antoni. You should continue straight on though where you'll soon pass through an iron gate and then later on a wooden gate.** Continue cycling along this route with the Santa Águeda on your left, a castle built on the site of an ancient Arabian fortress which stands 260 m/853 ft above sea level. **Keep right at the next junction ignoring the entrance to the Son Rubí estate on your left.** You will now join a tarmac path which takes you over a bridge to a crossroads where you can go left to Binimel·là beach, and right to Es Mercadal. **You should continue straight on for a while until you reach the next large T-junction where you turn left. Continue along the tarmac stretch known as Camí des Far, or "lighthouse path" for a further 6 km/3.7 miles** – past the excavation site Ciutat Romana de Sanitja (currently not open to the public) – to the remotely situated ❸ **Cap de Cavalleria → p. 57.** Explore the area around the (no access) **lighthouse!** The side facing east where the cliffs look as if someone chipped away at them with an axe offers particularly spectacular views.

11:00am Then return along the road you took to the ❹ **car park (approx. 4 km/2.5 miles away)** where you will see the start of the hiking path signposted. Lock up your bike and head off on foot towards the coast. One of the path's highlights already awaits you at the start of your walk: **climb down the steps to the ❺ Platja de Cavalleria,** a stunning double-crescent golden beach which is ideal for

16 km/10 mi

❸ Cap de Cavalleria

4 km/2.5 mi

❹ car park

1 km/0.6 mi

❺ Platja de Cavalleria

a spot of bathing! Then climb back up the steps and follow the picturesque coastal path to **⑥ Cala Binimel·là →** p. 57. This red sandy beach is also a perfect location to enjoy a swim. If you have worked up an appetite, head to the shady garden restaurant **Binimel·là** *(closed Nov–April | tel. 9 71 35 92 75 | Moderate–Expensive)* serving the best Menorcan cuisine. **Then follow the coastal path for another 20 minutes to ⑦ Cala Pregonda** with its bizarre rock formations. It's worth taking the same route back to the car park to enjoy the spectacular views.

03:00pm Now it's time to climb back on your bike **and cycle back southwards along the Camí des Far to the T-junction (approx. 3 km/1.9 mile away) where you bear left. After 1 km/0.6 mile shortly before reaching Ses Cases Noves, your route takes you right along another path through green plains. After 3 km/1.9 mile you'll reach another road** which you follow left back to **⑧ Es Mercadal →** p. 58. Take a well-earned break in this "culinary paradise" – there are plenty of restaurants to choose from – before climbing on your bike again. **Now head west along the busy Me-1 for just 500 m/1640 ft, turning right down the INSIDER TIP** *Camí d'en Kane*. This narrow romantic road, named after the British governor who ordered its construction in the 18th century, takes you past farmhouses along a picturesque hilly landscape. **After just 6 km/3.7 miles it merges into the Me-1 which will bring you straight back to ⑥ Ferreries (a further 2 km/1.2 mile).**

3 km/1.9 mi

⑥ Cala Binimel·là

2 km/1.2 mi

⑦ Cala Pregonda

14 km/8.7 mi

⑧ Es Mercadal

9 km/5.6 mi

⑥ Ferreries

---

④ UNSPOILT NATURE: HIKE IN ES GRAU

START: ⑥ Sa Mesquida END: ⑥ Sa Mesquida	½ day Walking time (without stops) approx. 4 ½ hours
Distance: easy ⟷ 17 km/11 mi ▪ll Height: 350 m/1148 ft	

COSTS: Approx. 20 euros for food in Es Grau
WHAT TO PACK: Swimwear, headwear, plenty of drinking water, comfortable shoes, picnic, if you'd like

IMPORTANT TIPS: The starting point is only accessible by car. Other sections of the route are highlighted red along the GR-223 hiking path.

The wetlands of S'Albufera des Grau represent the centrepiece of Menorca's biosphere reserve – an ecosystem encompassing forests, meadows, marshes and lakes. The area is also home to ducks, geese, osprey and heron. This hiking tour takes you over several passes, along the coast and down to the area's vast freshwater lagoon. There is also time for a spot of bathing at a beach along the way.

1 Sa Mesquida

2.3 km/1.4 mi

2 Macar de Binillautí

1.2 km/0.7 mi

3 Caleta de Binillautí

3 km/1.9 mi

4 Punta de sa Gola

0.8 km/0.5 mi

5 Platja d'Es Grau

1.2 km/0.7 mi

6 Cala des Tamarells

2.5 km/1.6 mi

09:00am **Starting from the car park at 1 Sa Mesquida, walk in the direction of the beach and keep left. At the end of the beach, the path leads up to the first pass and then descends down to the neighbouring bay of 2 Macar de Binillautí** – *macar* is the term used in Menorca to describe a pebbly beach. **The path then ascends to a second pass and then down again to the bay of 3 Caleta de Binillautí.** You pass through rugged scenery with bare rocks alternating with flat steppe landscape. **Shortly after leaving the bay, the path takes a turn inland, over another pass and along meadows to the Me-5. Follow it right and after 600 m/2000 ft follow the sign to the Lagune S'Albufera. Cross a canal over a bridge and keep left at the next junction (signpost: "Mirador" = viewpoint).** Follow the wooden walkways, which protect the salt-loving plants underneath, down to the lakeside where you can often spot heron and even osprey.

Now head up a flight of steps to the panoramic hill viewpoint **4 Punta de sa Gola**, with the vast lagoon now at your feet: you are surrounded by hills behind you with the village of Es Grau nestled in the long bay stretching along the coast in front of you. **Climb down the steps and follow the walkway to the left.** The path leads you through a shady pine forest to the **5 Platja d'Es Grau** dunes where you can bathe in the refreshing, turquoise waters.

At the north of the beach, the GR-223 signpost directs you inland through the pine forest. En route you will pass another panoramic viewpoint offering a fantastic view of the slate black Cap de Favàritx and its lighthouse in the distance. The path then continues down to the **6 Cala des Tamarells,** a bay dominated by the old watchtower **Torre de Rambla.** You can spend hours on this stranded Robinson Crusoe beach – it is the ideal spot for sunbathing, a refreshing swim in the sea and a picnic.

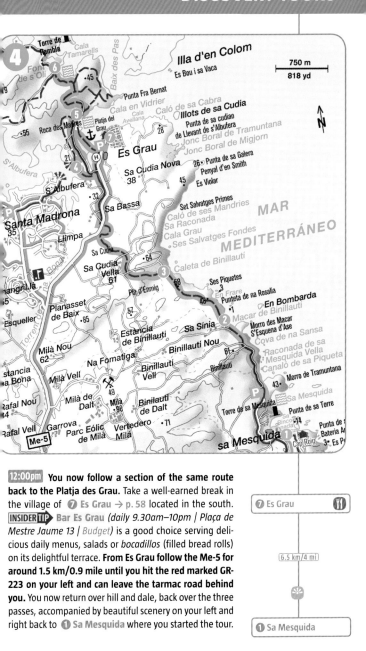

12:00pm You now follow a section of the same route back to the Platja des Grau. Take a well-earned break in the village of ❼ Es Grau → p. 58 located in the south. **INSIDER TIP** Bar Es Grau *(daily 9.30am–10pm | Plaça de Mestre Jaume 13 | Budget)* is a good choice serving delicious daily menus, salads or *bocadillos* (filled bread rolls) on its delightful terrace. **From Es Grau follow the Me-5 for around 1.5 km/0.9 mile until you hit the red marked GR-223 on your left and can leave the tarmac road behind you.** You now return over hill and dale, back over the three passes, accompanied by beautiful scenery on your left and right back to ❶ Sa Mesquida where you started the tour.

❼ Es Grau 🍴

(6.5 km/4 mi)

❶ Sa Mesquida

SPORTS & ACTIVITIES

For Menorcans sport is part of everyday life and even small children are happy to go off on hikes and to go for a bathe at least once a week because from May to October the sea is ideal for swimming, and the mild Mediterranean climate encourages outdoor activities all year round.

All the larger towns and resorts have modern sports facilities, not to mention private fitness clubs. For holidaymakers there are tennis and volleyball courts, mini golf, bicycle hire and water sport schools almost always in their own holiday resort on the coast. The "Menorca Activa" brochure is useful: *www.menorcaactiva.com.* Those looking for good spa facilities need deeper pockets, because facilities can be found only in the four and five-star hotels.

CYCLING

Although Menorca at first sight appears flat, if you are not a fit and experienced cyclist you will soon feel the many ascents. The main roads are very busy, there are very few bicycle paths, and lots of minor roads are in a very poor condition. However, cycling can still be a real pleasure in certain areas. This includes the western and eastern parts of the island around Ciutadella and Maó. Bicycle and mountain bike hire is available in both towns and in almost all the holiday resorts. *Anthony's Bikes (C/ Xaloc | Alaior | www.anthonysbikes.com)*

If you prefer not to laze about on holiday, there is a lot on offer: swimming, horseback riding, diving, hiking and cycling

rents out mountain bikes; tips for bike routes can be found on *www.menorca.es*.

DIVING

The underwater world of Menorca is ideal for ⭐ *diving*, though it has to be said that the main attraction is not so much the richness of the marine life but rather the clear water which provides excellent visibility. There are also numerous underwater caves and lots of shipwrecks on the seabed. There are about 20 diving schools on the island. Trial sessions, a complete diver training programme and daily trips as well as the hire of diving equipment are all part of the standard range of diving centres in the main holiday resorts and larger ports. Perhaps the nicest diving centre is *Poseidon Diving School (in the Hostal Bahía | Cala Santandria | tel. 9 71 38 26 44 | www.bahia-poseidon.de/en)*.

HIKING & TREKKING

Many hotels have a ready supply of suggestions for walks for their guests. There are hiking trails all over the island, but they are rarely signposted and often blocked by walls, locked gates and thorny vegetation. Hiking or army maps (obtainable in bookshops) are very useful, but not always accurate. Hiking clubs and other institutions organise (usually in the off-peak seasons) hikes in which non-members can also participate (announcements in the daily press).

The 185 km/115-mile coastal path ⭐ *Camí de Cavalls (www.camideca valls360.com)* encircling the island has been restored and newly marked. You can join it from many points on the island. The former "horse path" was created in the Middle Ages as a patrol path in order to be able to defend the island from any point. It is a popular hiking route every time of year. And no wonder – it leads past cliffs and pine forests, secluded bays and pristine beaches, and always has views of the sea.

Guided hikes are organised by *Dia complert (mobile tel. 6 09 67 09 96)*, *Viatges Magón (tel. 9 71 35 13 00 | www.me norcabookingcentre.com)* and *Xauxa Menorca Reloaded (C/ Verge del Toro 10 | Es Mercadal | mobile tel. 6 85 74 73 08 | www.rutasmenorca.com)*. The INSIDER TIP hikes through the gorges of the Barranc d'Algendar *(Club Aventura | Hotel Cala Galdana | tel. 9 71 15 45 00)* are really fantastic.

HORSEBACK RIDING

More than a dozen public and private riding schools (mostly in the island's interior) offer lessons and trail rides. At *Cavalls Son Àngel (Camí d'Algaiarens | Ciutadella | mobile tel. 6 09 83 39 02 | www.cavallssonangel.com)* you can book one-hour to five-day hacks, mainly on the Camí de Cavalls. And if you prefer to just watch: The two racecourses *Hipódrom Municipal (Ctra. Maó–Sant Lluís | Sat 6pm in summer, Sun mornings in autumn)* and *Hipódrom Torre del Ram (Ciutadella | Urb. Torre del Ram | Sun 6pm)* organise trotting races every weekend.

SAILING

Sailing courses are offered in Fornells, Son Xoriguer and Maó. Larger yachts or sailing boats, also with a skipper, are available in the ports in Maó, Ciutadella, Fornells, Cala en Bosc and S'Algar. The best option is *Windsurf Fornells (mobile tel. 6 64 33 58 01 | www.windfornells. com)*. On presentation of a valid sailing licence, you can hire sailing yachts and motorboats in Maó, for example at *Nautic Fun (Moll de Llevant 57 | tel. 9 71 36 42 50 | www.nauticfunmenorca.com)*.

TENNIS

All the major hotels have their own courts and tennis coaches are usually also available. The public courts are also available to holidaymakers!

WATER SPORTS

In addition to diving, the other favourites are windsurfing and kayaking. Water skiing and paragliding are available in S'Algar and Cala en Bosc. Pedalos and smaller motorboats (without sailing licence) are available at most holiday beaches. You can hire kayaks and SUP surfboards in Cala Galdana, Son Xoriguer, Es Grau and Fornells. The latter in particular is great for voyages of discovery on the calm waters of the large INSIDER TIP bay of Fornells with a view of the wild cliffs. The guides at *Dia Complert (Av. Passeig Maritim 41 | mobile tel. 6 09 67 09 96 | www.diacomplert.com)* lead you through caves and to the most beautiful parts of the coastline on their INSIDER TIP great kayak tours – if you wish, you can also stop for a snorkelling or sunbathing break at interesting spots or secluded beaches. Additionally, they've been offering diving, flyboard and paddle surf excursions for more than twenty years.

WELLNESS

All of the newer four and five-star hotels offer spa facilities with massage pools, Jacuzzis as well as dry and wet saunas. These facilities are not always included in the price; you will always be charged extra for massages and treatments. The *Insotel Punta Prima Prestige (see p. 51)* offers the best spa on the island followed by *Occidental Menorca (see p. 51)* in the same resort. The city hotels *Port Ciutadella (see p. 84)* and *Port Mahón (see p. 45)* are the perfect way to combine a wellness and culture break.

Hiking around the island on the Camí de Cavalls with the roar of the sea always in your ears

TRAVEL WITH KIDS

Athough there are relatively few activities aimed at children part from the island's sand and sea, Menorca welcomes its young visitors with family-friendly services offered in most hotels. Many of the larger hotels and club sites are specially tailored for children. Childcare is provided and an entertainments team ensures games, sport and lots of fun activities.

However, outside the hotels child-centred facilities are rare and though you will find a playground in almost all public parks, you will look in vain for nappy changing facilities in restaurants. Kids' menus in restaurants usually consist of little else but spaghetti bolognese or french fries with ketchup. Bicycles and hire cars can be rented with child seats.

The small tourist trains, which are now in all the major holiday resorts, are an entertaining means of transport and the perfect way to explore your area.

There are special events for children on all the island's summer patron saint days, such as theatre, concerts, competitions and sport, which usually take place in the late afternoon. Gigantic papier maché puppets *(gigantes* and *capgrossos)* often parade through the resort afterwards. The festival programme is in the local newspaper or advertised outside on the day before the festival starts. Parts of the events include equestrian displays on the squares and in the narrow streets. But because of the crowds of people, these *jaleos* are not completely without their risks and you should avoid getting caught

Water fun, horse rides and ancient ruins: on Menorca you can take your children with you everywhere – and most of them will love it!

up in the throng, especially with small children and buggies. A better option are the *jaleos de ases* (processions with donkeys) in Ferreries and Es Migjorn Gran. Most children also enjoy being allowed to stay up late to watch the midnight firework displays. Boat tours can also make a very pleasant change, and there are trips along the coast with a break for a swim with the "Don Joan" from Port de Maó (*Líneas de la Cruz,* see p. 43). There are also swimming trips especially for youngsters from Cala en Bosc or all day tours with time on the beach from Ciutadella (*daily from 10am | information at the port*).

MAÓ/EASTERN TIP

FORT MARLBOROUGH ●
(131 E–F4) (*M K6*)

Dark corridors, flickering candlelight, the thunder of cannons – with a light and sound show, the old British fortifications transport visitors back to the 18th century.

INSIDER TIP Free admission on Mondays! From the parking lot, a long, shadeless path leads to the fort, better to drive right up to the entrance! *June–Oct Mon–Tue 10am–3pm, Wed–Sun 9.30am–7.30pm, April/May Tue–Sat 9.30am–3pm | admission 8 euros, children (8–15 years) 3.60 euros | Cala Sant Esteve (near Es Castell) | tel. 9 71 36 04 62*

MIGJORN/CENTRE & SOUTH

CENTRE ARTESANAL DE MENORCA ●
(128 B3) (*ⱳ F4*)

Es Mercadal has a central forum for artisans from all over the island. Here you can admire not only modern and traditional Menorcan craftsmanship in the form of calabash bottles, woven fabrics, pottery and ceramics, but you can also buy, if the fancy takes you – every piece is unique. You can also watch the craftsmen at work, which is very interesting especially for children. There is also a museum for Menorcan arts and crafts. *Mon–Fri 11am–2pm and 5–8pm, Sat 11am–2pm, March/April only in the morning, Nov–April closed | free admission | Av. del Metge Camps | Es Mercadal | tel. 9 71 15 36 44 | www.artesaniademenorca. com*

CENTRE DE GEOLOGÍA DE MENORCA
(127 E4) (*ⱳ E4*)

"Discover Menorca by its colours" is the name of the small exhibition showing engagingly what it is with all the red, black, white and ochre rocks on the island. *May–Sept Tue–Sun 10am–2pm, 6–8pm, Oct/Nov and March/April Tue–Sat 10am–2pm | free admission | C/ Mallorca 2 | Ferreries | www.geologiamenorca.com*

ES LLOC DE MENORCA (128 C5) (*ⱳ c5*)

At this large zoo near Alaior, children can visit kangaroos and emus, monkeys and lemurs as well as feed its goats, pigs and cows. At a bird of prey demonstration, all the features of the big birds are explained. Most animals live in species-appropriate, accessible enclosures or aviaries so you can get in contact with them easily. By the way, many of the exotic animals come from European animal rescue shelters. *March–Nov. daily 10am–4pm | admission 12.50 euros, children (3–12 years) 8.50 euros, up to 2 years free | Ctra. General, km 7.8 | www.llocde menorca.com*

SON MARTORELLET (127 E4) (*ⱳ E4*)

Do your kids love horses? Fantastic shows are shown here, for example the "Dancing Horses"; you can also watch the Menorcan horses at their training and, during the day, visit their stables. *Stables Mon, Thu/Fri 5pm, admission 6.50 euros, children 3.40 euros, evening shows Tue and Thu 8.30pm (June–Sept, on great demand also May and Oct), admission from 32.50 euros, children from 18.50 euros; tickets also online | Ctra. Cala Galdana, km 1.7 | tel. 9 71 373406 | www. sonmartorellet.com*

CIUTADELLA/WESTERN TIP

AQUA CENTER (126 A3) (*ⱳ A3*)

Menorca's largest water park offers long water slides, an "adventure river", a "black hole", whirlpool, bouncy castle, playground equipment, restaurant, a go-kart track and a crèche for small children. *May–Sept daily 10.30am–6.30pm | admission 20 euros, children 10 euros (free up to 3 years) | Cala'n Blanes, north-west of Ciutadella | Av. Principal, Urb. Los Delfines | www.aquacenter-menorca.com |*

AQUAROCK (126 B5) (*ⱳ B5*)

Pure water fun: Water slides from *tube* to *kamikaze*, a wave pool, jacuzzi, children's pools and a large go-kart track right next door. *In summer daily (except on Sat in May, June and Sept) 10.30am–6pm | admission 20 euros, children 11, go-kart from 21 euros | Carreró Cova d'es Moro 88 | Cala en Bosc | www.aquarock-menorca.com*

CAVALLS SON ÀNGEL ●

(126 C2) (*Ø C3*)

Guided horse rides for the whole family through the unspoilt nature of the north coast are provided by *Toni Bosch*. The starting point is the neat, small estate *Finques Son Àngel* with friendly staff and relaxed atmosphere. Excursions take you through quiet nature reserves to the coast. *1 hr approx. 22 euros | getting there: Ciutadella, direction Cala Morell, then Camí d'Algaiarens "La Vall", km 1 | Toni Bosch mobile tel. 6 49 48 80 98 | www.cavallssonangel.com*

PEDRERA DE S'HOSTAL ★

(126 C3) (*Ø C3*)

The half underground quarry museum near Ciutadella, developed out of an old limestone quarry, is an attractive place for exploring, picnics and games of hide and seek. A labyrinth of limestone blocks has been created especially for children. There's also a beautiful garden. In July and August, **INSIDER TIP** concerts and dance performances take place every Wednesday evening. *Daily 9.30am–2.30pm, May–Sept also Mon–Sat 4.30pm to sunset | admission 4 euros, children free | Camí vell, km 1 | Ciutadella|www.lithica.es*

SURF & SAIL

(126 B5) (*Ø B5*)

Learn how to sail or windsurf, how to glide over the waves on water skis or have fun on the water banana – and not just for adults: there are special courses for children too. *Son Xoriguer | tel. 9 71 38 72 85 | tel. 9 71 38 71 05 | www.surfsailmenorca.com*

Fun in the sun: a slide into some cool water

FESTIVALS & EVENTS

Actually it is said that the Menorcans, by Mediterranean standards, are rather restrained in character. But this is refuted every year in June when the St John festival in Ciutadella is a highlight of the festival calendar. Horses dash through the crowds, there is lots of laughter, dancing, flirting and drinking.

LOCAL FESTIVALS & EVENTS

MARCH/APRIL
Setmana Santa (Holy Week); Good Friday procession in Maó; on Easter Sunday choirs perform all over the island

APRIL
23: *Festa de Sant Jordi* (St George's Day); roses and books are sold on the market squares

MAY
8: *Festa de la Verge del Toro*; as the island's patron saint, the Holy Virgin of Monte Toro is venerated

MAY/JUNE
Pentecostés (Whitsuntide); trips into the countryside are typical, often combined with a family picnic

JUNE
INSIDER TIP *Diumenge des Be* (Sunday of the Sheep); the St John celebrations are launched with a procession of sheep. 23/24: ★ *Festes de Sant Joan*; highlight of the festival week with cavalcades *(caragols)*, concerts and fireworks. 29: *Festa de Sant Pere*; fishing festival with sailing regattas at Port de Maó

JULY
15/16: *Festa del Carme* in Maó, Ciutadella, Fornells; boat processions in honour of Our Lady of Mount Carmel 24/25, Es Castell: *Festa de Sant Jaume* in honour of St James with cavalcades, music and firework display at the port 3rd Sun, Es Mercadal: *Festa de Sant Martí* in honour of St Martin with processions and cavalcade End July–end Aug: *Matins de l'orgue*; free organ recitals in Maó in the Santa María church; additionally the *Festival de Música de Maó; festivaldemusicademao. com*

AUGUST
9 Aug–beginning of Sept: INSIDER TIP *Festival de Música d'Estiu* (summer music festival) held in the seminary in Ciutadella and an even more spec-

Quiet and restrained? No chance!
The many exuberant patron saints festivals
with cavalcades are typical of Menorca

tacular venue just outside the city, the former quarry *L'Hostal de Líthica (www. pedravivamenorca.com)*

First weekend, Es Migjorn Gran: **Festa de Sant Cristófol** in honour of St Christopher

2nd weekend, Alaior: **Festes de Sant Llorenç** in honour of St Lawrence; horse races, procession

3rd weekend, Sant Climent: **Festes de Sant Climent** in honour of St Clement, water fights, cavalcade

23–25, Ferreries: **Festes de Sant Bartomeu** in honour of St Bartholomew; cavalcades, fun fair

4th weekend, Sant Lluís: **Festes de Sant Lluís** in honour of St Louis, with floats, concerts, fun fair, fireworks

SEPTEMBER

7–9, Maó: ● **Festes de la Verge de Gràcia** in honour of the capital's patron saint, with procession, equestrian displays, masses and fireworks

Sept/Oct in Maó and Ciutadella: **Festival de Jazz** with international stars

NATIONAL HOLIDAYS

1 January	*Cap d'any,* New Year
6 January	*Tres Reis,* Epiphany
17 January	*Festa de Sant Antonii*
1 March	*Dia de les Illes Balears,* Balearics Day
March/April	Maundy Thursday; Good Friday
1 May	*Festa de Treball,* Labour Day
15 August	*L'Assumpció,* Assumption
12 October	*Dia de l'Hispanitat,* Discovery of America
1 November	*Tots Sants,* All Saints' Day
6 December	*Dia de la Constitució,* Contitution Day
8 December	*La Immaculada Concepció,* Immaculate Conception
25/26 Dec	*Nadal,* Christmas

LINKS, BLOGS, APPS & MORE

menorca-live.com This site calls itself the "essential online guide to island life", and with good reason. It contains a wealth of information with lots of suggestions what to do and the latest news about events on the island

www.visitmenorca.com The official site of the Menorca Hotel Association and it provides lots of other useful information

www.clickmenorca.com/en A good site for accomodation, restaurants and activities (Spanish/Englisch)

menorcadiferente.com/mapas-de-menorca Excellent collection of useful maps including an overview of the nature reserves and the hiking trails along the *Camí de Cavalls*

www.gobmenorca.com Official site of the environment protection group GOB *(Grup Balear d'Ornitologia)*. It may well contain lots of interesting information, but be aware that the English version has been created by Google translate and it is perhaps more worth reading for its hilarious English!

www.elpaladar.es On this website you can order typical Menorcan products such as wine or cheese online

www.beautybyanya.com A new business model that provides mobile beauty treatments from pedicures to facials and various massages: you can enjoy the treatment on the spot in every resort on the island – even in your hotel and on Sundays and public holidays

linesofescape.com/2017/06/why-you-should-visit-menorca.html Visit this blog for stunning impressions of the island and inspiration for photo ops

handluggageonly.co.uk/tag/menorca The Handluggage Only blog combines a travel diary, eye candy and insider tipps into a neat and helpful package

Regardless of whether you are still researching your trip or already on Menorca: these addresses will provide you with more information, videos and networks to make your holiday even more enjoyable

www.museudemenorca.com/en/blog Blog by the island museum with interesting news concerning archaeological finds and the like

www.facebook.com/menorca Facebook site where you can get the latest news, look at photos and swap opinions

droneandslr.com/travel-blog/spain/best-places-watch-sunset-menorca Dramatic sunsets over rugged cliffs – this short guide gives away the best spots to watch

VIDEOS

droneandslr.com/travel-blog/spain/explore-best-beaches-menorca Descriptions and video of Menorca's most beautiful beaches for days of blissful beach hopping

fotomenorca.blogspot.com Cheeky photo blog by Sergio Vargas, with lots of unusual motifs and outstanding photos (also black and white)

www.youtube.com/watch?v=3p6CUThsdoY A 7-minute video showing Menorca's charme in HD, a little shaky at times but nonetheless stunning imagery

www.youtube.com/watch?v=14RdU59fst8 Word has got round that Menorca also has lots of underwater attractions. If you don't believe it, have a look here

www.youtube.com/watch?v=GhRJAmHxbnM Menorca is also a fun place to be for everyone wanting to enjoy the good life – drone and GoPro capturing the best moments

APPS

Menorca Offline Map, Minorca Offline City Map and Menorca Map offline Good maps which can be used offline to navigate the island (iOS and Android)

Enjoy Menorca An Android app providing information on beaches, hiking trails (Camí de Cavalls) and points of interest

MyTrails Ideal app to track hiking, cycling and running routes. Includes tours and trails for Menorca and other Balearic islands

TRAVEL TIPS

ARRIVAL

Menorca is only about a two-hour flight away from all the major airports in central Europe. The best deals are those offered by charter flights, with or without a complete package, as well as part of special offers from the major tour organisers. But there are also scheduled flights (amongst others, Condor direct, Iberia or – much cheaper – its no-frills carrier Vueling via Barcelona) connecting the European mainland with the Aeroport de Menorca (5 km/3.1 miles southwest of Maó). Direct flights from the UK are available with *Monarch (www. monarch.co.uk)*, *easyJet (www.easyjet. com)*, *Ryanair (www.ryanair.com)* and *Jet 2 (jet2.com)*. From the airport you can get a bus, but most tour operators have their own transfer networks between the airport and the hotels.

RESPONSIBLE TRAVEL

It doesn't take a lot to be environmentally friendly whilst travelling. Don't just think about your carbon footprint whilst flying to and from your holiday destination but also about how you can protect nature and culture abroad. As a tourist it is especially important to respect nature, look out for local products, cycle instead of driving, save water and much more. If you would like to find out more about eco-tourism please visit: *www.ecotourism.org*

Travelling from France is best via the A7 Dijon–Lyon–Nîmes motorway through the Rhone Valley, then on the A9 to Perpignan, crossing into Spain at Figueres and then by ferry from Barcelona or València. Motorways in France and Spain are subject to charges.

Ferries sail from Barcelona and València several times a week, in summer more frequently, and their destination is Port de Maó *(approx. 8 hours)*. You can also use the cheap flights to neighbouring Mallorca and then take the Maó–Palma ferry *(only Sat/Sun, 6–7 hours | Trasmediterránea-Acciona | Maó | Moll Comercial | tel. 9 02 45 46 45 | www. trasmediterranea.es)*. Other connections: Alcúdia–Ciutadella *(approx. 3 hours | Iscomar | tel. 9 02 11 91 28 or from abroad 0034 9 71 43 75 00 | wwwiscomar.com)*, Alcúdia–Ciutadella/Maó *(fast car ferry | Baleària | tel. 9 02 16 01 80 | www.balea ria.com)*. Reservations are recommended in the summer season (May–Oct), especially if you're travelling by car from the mainland.

BANKS & CREDIT CARDS

Banks are usually only open 9am–1pm or 2pm, but bureaux de change in the tourist resorts are often open in the afternoon. There are numerous ATMs and credit cards are widely used and are accepted in almost all shops, hotels and restaurants. Card providers with the most extensive network on the island are VISA, Mastercard and Eurocard; American Express and Diners Club are not as yet widely accepted.

From arrival to weather

Your holiday from start to finish: the most important addresses and information for your trip to Menorca

BUSES

The public transport network is dominated by three companies: *TMSA (tel. 9 71 36 04 75 | www.tmsa.es)*, *Autos Fornells (mobile tel. 6 86 93 92 46 | www.autofornells.com)* and *Torres (tel. 9 71 38 64 61 | www.bus.e-torres.net)*. The network and the current bus timetables can be viewed at *www.menorca.tib.org*.

CAMPING

To find out whether or not camping is allowed, you need to check with the municipality or the respective property owner. Camping rough is prohibited as is camping in the nature reserves! There are two campsites: *S'Atalaia (May–Oct | Ferreries –Cala Galdana, km 4 | tel. 9 71 37 42 32 | www.campingsatalaia.com)*, 3 km/2 miles from the coast, in a pine forest between Ferreries and Cala Galdana, and *Son Bou (April–Oct | Ctra. de San Jaume, km 3.5 | tel. 9 71 37 27 27 | www.campingsonbou.com)* which has lots of opportunities for sport.

CAR

If not otherwise signposted, the maximum speed limit in built up areas is 50 km/30 mph, on main roads 80 km/50 mph but if there is a hard shoulder at least 1.5m wide, then 100 km/60 mph. Seatbelts are obligatory for both the front seat passenger and back seat passenger (if belts are fitted in the rear). Wearing a helmet is obligatory for moped and motorbike riders. Motorists must carry two reflective vests and two warning triangles in case of accident or breakdown; the use

BUDGETING

Coffee	£1.20–£1.90/ $1.6–$2.60 *for a latte in a café*
Menorcan cheese	£8–£15/$10–$19 *per kilo in a shop*
Wine	from £7/$9 *for a bottle in a restaurant*
Abarques	£13–£26/$17–$35 *for a pair of typical Menorcan sandals*
Fuel	around £1.3/$1.70 *for a litre of super*
Disco	£13–£22/$17–$29 *admission in the evening*

of a mobile phone without hands-free facility is strictly prohibited. And breathalyser tests are carried out more frequently; the drink drive limit is *0.5*.

People drive in Menorca with a certain Mediterranean nonchalance. This is particularly evident at pedestrian crossings which are largely ignored and at traffic lights where people are happy to race through on amber/red.

Super, diesel and lead free *(sin plomo)* and also Super or Extra lead free (98 octane) are available at eleven filling stations: in Maó (3), Ciutadella (3), Alaior (2), Sant Lluís, Es Mercadal and on the main Maó–Fornells road.

CAR AND (MOTOR)CYCLE HIRE

You can hire a car at the airport and in all the major tourist resorts. You will find bicycles in almost all the holiday resorts, but motorcycles only in Ciutadella and Maó. The cheapest provider far and wide is INSIDER TIP ▶ *Tramuntana (tel. 6 50 65 70 45 | tramuntanarentacar.es)*, where you can get a rental car for a week from 15 euros per day (a car for one day costs from 35 euros). The service is unbeatable as well: The car is brought to every place on the island without any surcharge; you don't have to pay extra for a second driver, and there are no tricks when the tank is filled.

Bikes from mountain bike to trekking adnd racing bikes can be hired at *Bike Menorca* in *Maó (Av. Francesc Femenías 44 | www.bikemenorca.com)*. *Velos Joan (www.velosjoan.com)* has branches in Maó and Ciutadella.

CONSULATES & EMBASSIES

UK HONORARY VICE CONSULATE
Cami Biniatap, 30 | Horizonte | tel. +34 902 109 356 | Mon–Fri 10am–midday

US CONSULATE
There is no consulate on Menorca, but there is one on Mallorca: *c/Porto Pi, 8–9D | Palma de Mallorca | tel. +34 971 40 37 07 | Mon–Fri 10.30am–1.30pm | es.usembassy. gov/u-s-citizen-services/u-s-consular-offic es/consular-agency-palma-de-mallorca*

CUSTOMS

For adult EU citizens the following duty free allowances apply (import and export): for own consumption 800 cigarettes, 90l win, 10l spirits.

Travellers to the US who are residents of the country do not have to pay duty on articles purchased overseas up to the value of $800, but there are limits on the amount of alcoholic beverages and tobacco products. For the regulations for

international travel for US residents please see *www.cbp.gov*

ELECTRICITY

The mains voltage in all hotels and hostels is 230 volts, but British electrical items will work with the correct travel plug adaptor to convert the UK standard 3 pin to Spanish 2 pin socket. North American visitors should also bring a transformer.

EMERGENCIES

In an emergency, phone *112* whatever the problem. This service is also available in English. If you lose your bank or credit card, contact your bank in the UK immediately and report the theft to the police. Make sure you have made a note of your card company's 24-hour contact phone number before you go away. If your cards are registered with a card protection agency, ensure you have their contact number and your policy number with you.

HEALTH

Chemists *(farmacias)* are indicated with a green cross – usually as a neon light. When closed, a notice displays the nearest emergency chemist.

In the case of illness, the EHIC (European Health Insurance Card) card is valid. American visitors are advised to ensure they have health insurance. Medical services often have to be paid for in cash, in which case it is important to get a receipt *(recibo oficial)* from the doctor (also for expensive medicines or dental treatment) so that you can be reimbursed.

In the holiday resorts there are special *centros médicos* which are equipped to deal with medical needs, communication problems and the most common holiday illnesses. Dentists are listed under *dentista*. You can call for an ambulance day and night on *tel. 061*.

IMMIGRATION

Visitors from Britain will need a valid passport – even though it is no longer checked on immigration from Schengen countries – and should have it on you at all times in the case of police checks (for motorists), when notifying a theft etc. Tourists from the USA, Canada and Australia do not need a visa for stays under 90 days.

INFORMATION

SPANISH TOURIST OFFICE TURESPAÑA

– *64 North Row| W1K 7DE, London | tel. 020 7317 2011 | www.spain.info*
– *845 North Michigan Av, Suite 915-E | Chicago IL 60611| tel. 312 642 1992| www.spain.info/en_US*
– *60 East 42nd Street, Suite 5300 | New York NY 10165-0039| tel. 212 265 8822| www.spain.info/en_US*

OFICINA DE INFORMACIÓN TURÍSTICA

– *Maó (Plaça Constitució 22 | tel. 9 71 35 59 52)*
– *Ciutadella (Plaça d'es Born 15 | tel. 9 71 48 41 55)*

You can get on the spot assistance and information not only at the two tourist offices in Maó and Ciutadella, but also at the information booth at the airport *(arrivals hall | only in the summer)*, the office at the Port de Maó *(Moll de Llevant 2 | tel. 9 71 35 59 52)* as well as a mobile support office which visits the main resorts for one day each in summer. General information: *www.menorca.es, www.tourspain.es, www.visitmenorca.com, www.visitbalears.com* or from the call

centre: *tel. 9 71 35 59 52*. If you speak Spanish, this social media platform allows locals and tourists to have their say: *www.menorca.info*.

INTERNET & WIFI

The island's government launched a free 30-minute WiFi service accessible in all larger resorts. A free Internet service will also soon be available on all the island's beaches! Log on to the Internet at *www.menorcawifi.com* where online access costs approx. 5 euros for a day. Many bars (usually cafés) and hotels (nearly always in the reception area) have also set up small WiFi zones where visitors have to ask at the reception or the restaurant owner for the access code: "Cual es la clave de la red inalambrica?" You will be charged for use more frequently here than on the Spanish mainland (3–6 euros a day). Your travel operator or porter can provide more information.

Internet cafés are few and far between. There is one in Ciutadella *(Plaça des Pins 37)* and one in Maó *(C/ Nou 25)*.

LANGUAGE

You can get by quite well on Menorca with English, but Spanish *(castellano)* is, of course, even better. If you'd like to surprise your host with a few words in *català*, you will find a few expressions in the "Useful Phrases", p. 120. But remember that there are some differences between the *menorquí* dialect and Catalan.

NEWSPAPERS

All the important mass circulation English daily and weekend newspapers as well as magazines are available on Menorca,

CURRENCY CONVERTER

£	€	€	£
1	1.14	1	0.88
3	3.43	3	2.63
5	5.70	5	4.38
13	14.85	13	11.38
40	46	40	35
75	86	75	66
120	137	120	105
250	286	250	219
500	571	500	438

$	€	€	$
1	0.81	1	1.23
3	2.43	3	3.70
5	4.05	5	6.17
13	10.54	13	16.04
40	32.42	40	49.35
75	61	75	92.52
120	97	120	148
250	203	250	308
500	405	500	617

For current exchange rates see www.xe.com

in the morning. In peak season (mid-May–Feb), most restaurants are open daily, from lunchtime around noon to 10 or 11 in the evening. (Opening times in this guide refer to peak season, if not otherwise stated.) In the off-season, many hotels are closed and many restaurants are not open daily, so you should check the current opening times beforehand on the restaurant's website..

PHONE & MOBILE PHONE

The international dialling code for Spain is *+34*, followed by the 9-digit number. For the UK *+44* and for the US and Canada *+1*. You can phone home from every telephone booth which is marked *internacional*. The cabins also accept the practical telephone cards, *teletarjeta*, which are sold at newspaper kiosks. In telephone and Internet shops *(locutorios)* you will be charged at the end of your call.

Your mobile phone can be used without any problems. EU citizens don't pay any more for their calls than at home.

POST

Postage for letters and postcards to the rest of Europe is currently 1.25 euros. You can buy stamps at the post office and in all the tobacconists identified with the national colours; post offices are only open in the mornings (in Maó all day). The main post offices are: *Alaior (C/ Forn 1), Es Castell (C/ Llevant), Ciutadella (Pl. des Born 5), Maó (C/ Bonaire 15)*.

PRICES

Compared with prices on the mainland, those on the island are a little higher, especially for lots of foodstuffs. The admission fee for museums is between 3–6

but usually with one or two days delay. There is no English newspaper especially for holidaymakers such as is available on Mallorca and Ibiza.

NUDIST BEACHES

In contrast to the other Balearic islands, Menorca has no designated nudist beaches. But topless bathing is tolerated on all beaches and in small, hidden away bays people also sunbathe in the nude.

OPENING TIMES

Normally, shops are open Mon–Fri 9am–1.30pm and 5–8pm, on Saturdays only euros, the set menu in an average restaurant costs 15–30 euros.

An accomodation tax is slapped on the hotel price in peak season (May–Oct) per night per guest over 16. It is meant to help with nature protection. The amount depends on the hotel category; it starts at 2 euros.

RADIO

Radio One Mallorca is a 24-hour English radio station with lots of news, events, fiestas, local personalities and more. Though based in Mallorca, it also promotes events on Menorca and is available via radio (97.7 FM on Menorca), on the internet and via mobile phones. *www. radioonemallorca.com*

TAXIS

You can find taxis even in the smaller towns, usually at a designated taxi rank. Should there be no taxi waiting there, the taxi headquarters will help. *Maó: tel. 9 71 36 71 11 | Ciutadella: tel. 9 71 48 22 22*

TELEVISION

Almost all the hotels have satellite dishes and receive programmes in English.

TIPPING

Rule of thumb: 5–10 per cent of the bill are appropriate for waiters in a restaurant. Room maids, porters, taxi drivers and guides are also pleased when they receive a tip.

WEATHER IN MAÓ

	Jan	Feb	March	April	May	June	July	Aug	Sept	Oct	Nov	Dec
Daytime temperatures in °C/°F	14/57	14/57	16/61	18/64	21/70	25/77	28/82	28/82	26/79	22/72	18/64	14/57
Nighttime temperatures in °C/°F	7/45	7/45	9/48	11/52	13/55	17/63	20/68	20/68	19/66	15/59	11/52	9/48
Sunshine hours/day	5	5	6	8	10	10	12	10	8	6	5	4
Precipitation days/month	9	8	8	7	5	3	1	3	6	11	9	12
Water temperature in °C/°F	14/57	13/55	14/57	14/57	17/63	20/68	23/73	25/77	23/73	21/70	18/64	15/59

☀ Sunshine hours/day 🌂 Precipitation days/month ≋ Water temperature in °C/°F

USEFUL PHRASES CATALAN

PRONUNCIATION

c	like "s" before "e" and "i" (e.g. Barcelona); like "k" before "a", "o" and "u" (e.g. Casa)
ç	pronounced like "s" (e.g. França)
g	like "s" in "pleasure" before "e" and "i"; like "g" in "get" before "a", "o" and "u"
l·l	pronounced like "l"
que/qui	the "u" is always silent, so "qu" sounds like "k" (e.g. perquè)
v	at the start of a word and after consonants like "b" (e.g. València)
x	like "sh" (e.g. Xina)

IN BRIEF

Yes/No/Maybe	Sí/No/Potser
Please/Thank you/Sorry	Sisplau/Gràcies/ Perdoni
May I...?	Puc ...?
Pardon?	Com diu *(Sie)*?/Com dius *(Du)*?
I would like to.../	Voldria.../
Have you got...?	Té...?
How much is...?	Quant val...?
I (don't) like this	(no) m'agrada
good	bo/bé *(Adverb)*
bad	dolent/malament *(Adverb)*
Help!/Attention!/Caution!	Ajuda!/Compte!/Cura!
ambulance	ambulància
police/fire brigade	policia/bombers
Prohibition/forbidden	prohibició/prohibit
danger/dangerous	perill/perillós
May I take a photo here/of you?	Puc fer-li una foto aquí?

GREETINGS, FAREWELL

Good morning!/afternoon!	Bon dia!
Good evening!/night!	Bona tarda!/Bona nit!
Hello!/Goodbye!	Hola!/Adéu! Passi-ho bé!
See you	Adéu!
My name is...	Em dic...
What's your name?	Com es diu?

Parles Català?

"Do you speak Catalan?" This guide will help you to say the basic words and phrases in Catalan

DATE & TIME

Monday/Tuesday	dilluns/dimarts
Wednesday/Thursday	dimecres/dijous
Friday/Saturday	divendres/dissabte
Sunday/working day	diumenge/dia laborable
holiday	dia festiu
today/tomorrow/	avui/demà/
yesterday	ahir
hour/minute	hora/minut
day/night/week	dia/nit/setmana

TRAVEL

open/closed	obert/tancat
entrance/driveway	entrada
exit/exit	sortida
departure/	sortida/
departure/arrival	sortida d'avió/arribada
toilets/restrooms /	Lavabos/
ladies/gentlemen	Dones/Homes
Where is...?/	On està...?/
Where are...?	On estan...?
left/right	a l'esquerra/a la dreta
close/far	a prop/lluny
bus	bus
taxi/cab	taxi
bus stop/	parada/
cab stand	parada de taxis
parking lot/	aparcament/
parking garage	garatge
street map/map	pla de la ciutat/mapa
train station/harbour	estació/port
airport	aeroport
schedule/ticket	horario/bitllet
train / platform/track	tren/via
platform	andana
I would like to rent...	Voldria llogar...
a car/a bicycle	un cotxe/una bicicleta
petrol/gas station	gasolinera
petrol/gas / diesel	gasolina/gasoil
breakdown/repair shop	avaria/taller

FOOD & DRINK

Could you please book a table for tonight for four?	Voldriem reservar una taula per a quatre persones per avui al vespre
on the terrace	a la terrassa
The menu, please	la carta, sisplau
Could I please have...?	Podria portar-me...?
bottle/carafe/glass	ampolla/garrafa/got
salt/pepper/sugar	sal/pebrot/sucre
vinegar/oil	vinagre/oli
vegetarian/	vegetarià/vegetariana/
allergy	allèrgia
May I have the bill, please?	El compte, sisplau

SHOPPING

Where can I find...?	On hi ha...?
I'd like.../	voldria/
I'm looking for...	estic buscant...
pharmacy/chemist	farmacia/drogueria
baker/market	forn/mercat
shopping center	centre comercial/gran magatzem
supermarket	supermercat
kiosk	quiosc
expensive/cheap/price	car/barat/preu
organically grown	de cultiu ecológic

ACCOMMODATION

I have booked a room	He reservat una habitació
Do you have any... left?	Encara té...
single room	una habitació individual
double room	una habitació doble
breakfast/half board	esmorzar/mitja pensió
full board	pensió completa
at the front/seafront	exterior/amb vistes al mar
shower/sit down bath	dutxa/bany
balcony/terrace	balcó/terrassa

BANKS, MONEY & CREDIT CARDS

bank/ATM	banc/caixer automàtic
pin code	codi secret
cash/	al comptat/
credit card	amb targeta de crèdit
change	canvi

HEALTH

doctor/dentist/paediatrician	metge/dentista/pediatre
hospital/emergency clinic	hospital/urgència
fever/pain	febre/dolor
inflamed/injured	inflamat/ferit
plaster/bandage	tireta/embenat
ointment/cream	pomada/crema
pain reliever/tablet	analgèsic/pastilla

POST, TELECOMMUNICATIONS & MEDIA

stamp/letter/postcard	segell/carta/ postal
I need a landline phone card	Necessito una targeta telefònica per la xarxa fixa
I'm looking for a prepaid card for my mobile	Estic buscant una targeta de prepagament pel mòbil
Where can I find internet access?	On em puc connectar a Internet?
Do I need a special area code?	He de marcar algun prefix determinat?
socket/adapter/charger	endoll/adaptador/carregador
computer/battery/ rechargeable battery	ordinador/bateria/ acumulador
at sign (@)	arrova
internet address	adreça d'internet (URL)
e-mail address	adreça de correu electrònic
e-mail/file/print	correu electrònic/fitxer/imprimir

LEISURE, SPORTS & BEACH

beach	platja
sunshade/lounger	para-sol/gandula

NUMBERS

0 zero	12 dotze	60 seixanta
1 un/una	13 tretze	70 setanta
2 dos/dues	14 catorze	80 vuitanta
3 tres	15 quinze	90 noranta
4 quatre	16 setze	100 cent
5 cinc	17 disset	200 dos-cents/dues-centes
6 sis	18 divuit	1000 mil
7 set	19 dinou	2000 dos mil
8 vuit	20 vint	10000 deu mil
9 nou	30 trenta	
10 deu	40 quaranta	½ mig
11 onze	50 cinquanta	¼ un quart

ROAD ATLAS

The green line indicates the Discovery Tour "Menorca at a glance"
The blue line indicates the other Discovery Tours

All tours are also marked on the pull-out map

Photo: Cows in the island's interior

Exploring Menorca

The map on the back cover shows how the area has been sub-divided

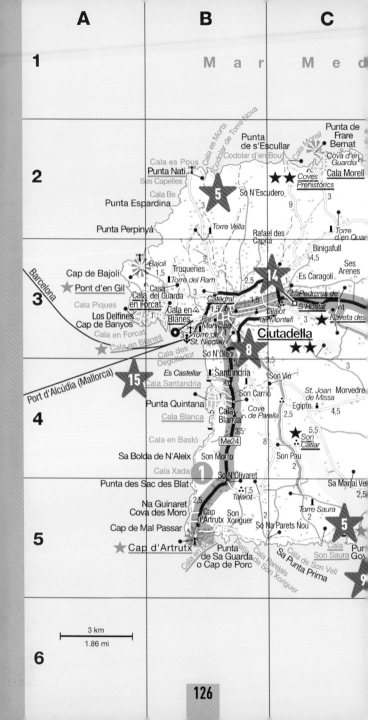

D   E   F

errània

1

I. DES PORROS
Es Pas
Port de Sanitja
Cala Torta
Punta des Vernís
Platja de Ferragut
Cala Mica
Santa Te

Cap Gros
Recó des Llenyam
Cala en Carbó
I. BLEDES
Cala en Caldes
Cala Barril
Cala Pregonda
Sa Falconera
Cala Moragues
Cala del Pilar
Es Piló
Chalets de
So N'Ametler
So N'Ermità
So N'Ametler
Escolló del Francés
2
Sa Muntanya Mala
205
So N'Ermità
Binimel·la
La Vall
2,5
Santa Elisabet
3 Binimel la Nou
Sant Félip
4,5
Ses Cases N
Sa Font Santa
Santa Agueda
3
4,5
S'Almudaina
Castell de
Santa Agueda
260
5,5
3
on Planes
Alqueria Blanca
1
169
27
Binisues
3,5
Montenegro
3
1
3
Ses Tavernes
191
3
Sintes
Son Toni Martí
Santa Bàrbara
3,5
uda
re Trencada
2
S'Enclùsa
275
★ Es Mercadal
a Trencada
7,5
So N'Arro
Me1
Pas d'En Revull
Ferreries
Ermita
Torre Petxina
(80) 2
Me18
Naveta
4,5
Sa Roca
Me22
7
Ses Fontsredones
237
Me16
4,5
4,5
3
Migjorn Gran
Santa Ponça
Es Migjorn
Gran
4
Santa Ana
Son Mercer de Baix
(111)
1
Binicudrell
Me18
10
Serpentona
7
Cala Santa
Galdana
Cova dels
Coloms
S'Enfonsat de Binisaid
Cova Polida
5
136
Sant Agustí
Torre Soli
2
Sant Adeodat
5
Punta Rabiosa
Sant Tomás
Sant Jaume
Mediterrani
Platja Sant Tomás
9
Punta Negra
Punta d'Atalitx
Platges de Son Bou
Son Bou
MENORCA
Cap de ses Penyes
6
Cala de Llucalari
Cala de St. Llo

A   **B**   Barcelona   **C**

12

1   *I. DES PORROS*   **3**   **Cap de Cavalleria** ★★

Es Pas   Cap Roig

Port de Sanitja   Punta d'en Baptista

Cala Torta   *Cala Viola*

BLEDES   **Punta des Vernis**   *Sa Nitja*

Platja de Ferragut   **Na Guillem**

Barril   **Santa Teresa**   **Sa Trona**   *Cova dels An*

Piló   **Chalets de**   *Cala Mica*   **Punta**   **Cap de Fornells**   *Cova Polida* Morro

So N'Ametler   **Negra**   ★ *Torre del*   **1**   **Fornells**   Pun

Escollo   **Binimel·la**   *Fornells*

2   **del Francés**   **Cala**   *Coves N*

3 Binimel la Nou   **Tirant**   Platges   **Es Niu**

de   *Fornells*   *Cala Pude*

stell de   2,5   *Arenal de*

nta Agueda   **Ses Cases Noves**   **Ses Salines**   *Cala*   **Cap**

2,5   1,5   *Blanca*   *Are*

10   ★ **Son Parc**   *d'e*

1,5   **3**   2,5   **5**   *cas*

5,5   3   2   **Arenal**

3   **3**   Me7   1,5   **d'en Cast**

169   Me15   7   **Ses**

Montenegro   **Sant Joan**   **Coves**

3   *des Horts*   **Llucaitx**   **Velles**   *Cal*

3   2   *Se*

★ **Es Mercadal**   **Sa Roca**   *Hort de*   *M*

7,5   (60)   **4**   *Mare de Déu*   *Llucaitx*

So N'Arro   Me1   *del Toro*   2   4

Ermita   ○ *337*   *Puig de S'Albaida*

Naveta   Me18   **El Toro**   **Santa Eulària**   *172*

Sa Farinera   **d'Alt**   *S'Albaida*

4   **Ses Fontsredones**   *Sa Roca de S'Indio*   *Camí d'en Kane*   5   **Son Gall**

237   6

Migjorn Gran   3   4,5   **S'Artiga Vella**

er   **Es Migjorn**   Me16   Me1

Gran   (111)

Coves de   *S'Encantament*   □ *Cementiri*

Binicudrell   Me18   1   1,5

2   *Cova dels*   **1**   1,5

Coloms   ✈   (130)   1,5   ★ **Alaior**

va Polida   *Sant Agustí*   3   **Llucassaldent**   1,5

5   **Sant Adeodat**   2,5   3   **24**

Torre Soli   **La Arge**   5,5

Sant Tomás   **136** ▲   5   2,5

1,5   **Sant Jaume**   ★★ *Torralba*   **6**

Punta Negra   **Mediterrani**   1,5   ★★ *d'en Salort*

Punta d'Atalitx   **Sant Jaume**   4,5

★ *Platges de Son Bou*   *Llucalari*

★★ *Torre*   3,5

Son Bou   *Básilica*   *d'en Galmés*

Cap de ses Penyes   *Paleocristiana*   4

Cala de Llucalari   **Sant Llorenç**   *Torre Llissa*

5   *So na Caçar*

Cala de St. Llorenç   **Cala en Porter**   *Biniadrix*   *M*

2

6   ▽ *130*   **9**   **128**   **Cala En**   ★ *Cales*   **Son Vitam**

Porter   *Coves*   **del Mar**

Cova d'en Xaroi   *Cova*

Mar Mediterrània

3 km
1.86 mi

Pantiné

Joanassa
Punta Codolar
Cala es Morts
Ricó d'en Ferradura
I. PETITA D'ADDAIA
I. GRAN D'ADDAIA
Na Macaret ★
Macar Real
en Brut
d'Addaia
Sibinar de Montgofre
Cala Cáldes
Punta Timons
Es Portitxol
Cap de Favàritx ★★ ★ **11**
Cala Presili

Pàre
Capifort
·81
Capifort
7,5
Cala Morella Nou
Cap de Monsenyor Vives

Na La
Morella Vell
Llosar de Rambla
de Sa Torreta
I. D'EN COLOM
Me7
Torre Blanca
Sa Torreta
Cap de Llevant

NaVermella
de s'Albufera
S.Albufera
Platja d'es Grau
ILLOTS DE SA CUDIA

Menor
·112
Mare de
Déu de Fatima
13
Es Grau
Punta de sa Galera

Santa Madrona
4,5
Caló de ses Màndries

Shangri-La
Sa Cudia
Torreta
Caleta de Binillautí

Son Cardona
i d'en Kane
4
5
Es Pa Gros
Sa Mesquida

Me5
94
Mila
Sa Mesquida
2,5
Es Murtar

Me1
Sa Granya
2
Golden Farm
Cap Negre

i de Dalt
Sant Joan dels
Vergers
Museu
Sant Antoni
2,5
Cala
Llonga

Algendar
Basilica
de's Fornàs
Me14
Santa
Maria
I. DEL REI
La Mola

Talaiot
Teatre
Principal
El Fonduco
I. DEL
LLATZERET
4
Fortalesa
de Isabel II
Punta de S'Esperó

Climent
Mao
Me8
Es Castell
Sinia
Riera
Santa
Ana
131

Aeroport de
Menorca
1
3
★ ★
Talaiot
5 de
Trepucó
129
Cast. de
St. Felip
Punta de Sant Carles

Llucmaçanes
1,5
1,5
Cala Sant Esteve

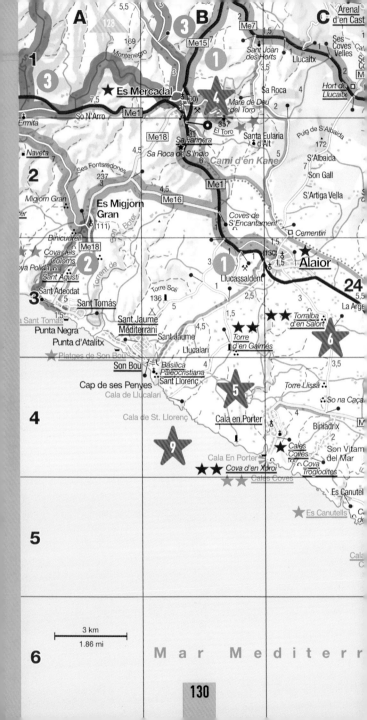

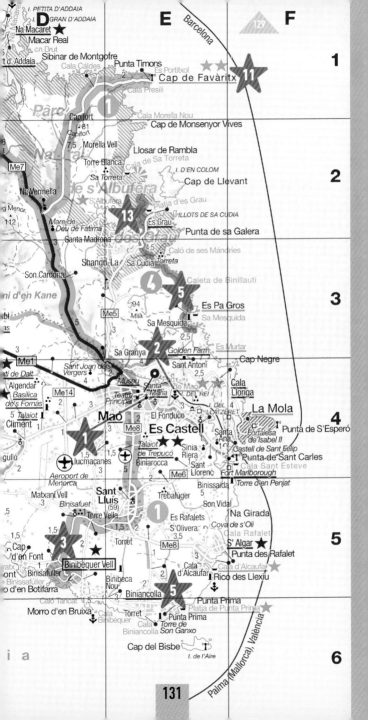

I. PETITA D'ADDAIA
I GRAN D'ADDAIA

D   **E**   Barcelona   **F**

129

Na Macaret ★
Macar Real
en Drut
d'Addaia
Sibinar de Montgofre
Cala Caldes
Punta Timons
Es Portixol   ★ ★   **11**
Cap de Favàritx

Parc   Capifort
Cala Presili

Cala Morella Nou

Capifort
81
Capitort
7,5   Morella Vell
Cap de Monsenyor Vives

Me7
Torre Blanca
Llosar de Rambla
Cala de Sa Torreta

Sa Torreta
I. D'EN COLOM
Cap de Llevant

Na Vermella
de s'Albufera
S'Albufera
Platja d'es Grau

g Menor
112
Mare de
Déu de Fàtima
13
Es Grau
ILLOTS DE SA CUDIA

Santa Madrona
Punta de sa Galera

4,5
Caló de ses Mánories

Shangri-La   Sa Cudia   Torreta
Caleta de Binillauti

Son Cardona
4   **5**

ni d'en Kane
94
Mila
Es Pa Gros
Sa Mesquida

bl
Me5
Sa Mesquida

as
5
2,5

3
Me1
Sa Granya   **2**   Golden Farm   Es Murtar

ati de Dalt
Sant Joan des
Vergers
Sant Antoni
Cap Negre

Algendar
Museu
Santa
Maria
2,5
Cala
Llonga

Basílica
des Fornàs
Teatre
Principal
I. DEL REI

5   Talaiot
Climent
Mao   El Fonduco
I. DEL
LLATZERET
La Mola

Fortalesa
de Isabel II
Punta de S'Esperó

gulló
1   Me8   **Es Castell**
Santa
Ana
Castell de Sant Felip

Llucmaçanes   Talaiot
de Trepucó   ★ ★   Sinia
Riera   Punta de Sant Carles
Cala Sant Esteve

Aeroport de
Menorca
Biniarocca
Sant
Llorenç
Fort Marlborough

Matxaní Vell   Me6
Binissaida   Torre d'en Penjat

Binisafuet
**Sant
Lluis**
(59)
Trebalúger
Son Vidal
Na Girada
Cova de s'Oli
Cala Rafalet

,5
Torre Vella
1
Es Rafalets
S'Olivera
3,5
S' Algar   ★

Cap
d'en Font
Torret
Me8
Punta des Rafalet

Binisafuller   **3**   2   Cala
d'Alcaufar
Cala d'Alcaufar

ont
Binibèquer Vell
Rico des Llexiu

o d'en Botifarra
Binibeca
Nou
5
Punta Prima

Morro d'en Bruixa   Torret   Punta Prima
Platja de Punta Prima

Caló Tancat
Cala
Binibèquer
Biniancolla
Torre de
Son Ganxo

Cap del Bisbe
I. de l'Aire

i a

131

Palma (Mallorca), València

1

2

3

4

5

6

KEY TO ROAD ATLAS

Autobahn · Gebührenpflichtige Anschlussstelle · Gebührenstelle · Anschlussstelle mit Nummer · Rasthaus mit Übernachtung · Raststätte · Kleinraststätte · Tankstelle · Parkplatz mit und ohne WC	Trento · ⑪	Motorway · Toll junction · Toll station · Junction with number · Motel · Restaurant · Snackbar · Filling-station · Parking place with and without WC
Autobahn in Bau und geplant mit Datum der voraussichtlichen Verkehrsübergabe	Datum ... Date	Motorway under construction and projected with expected date of opening
Zweibahnige Straße (4-spurig)		Dual carriageway (4 lanes)
Fernverkehrsstraße · Straßennummern	14 E45	Trunk road · Road numbers
Wichtige Hauptstraße		Important main road
Hauptstraße · Tunnel · Brücke	)=(	Main road · Tunnel · Bridge
Nebenstraßen		Minor roads
Fahrweg · Fußweg		Track · Footpath
Wanderweg (Auswahl)		Tourist footpath (selection)
Eisenbahn mit Fernverkehr		Main line railway
Zahnradbahn, Standseilbahn		Rack-railway, funicular
Kabinenschwebebahn · Sessellift		Aerial cableway · Chair-lift
Autofähre · Personenfähre		Car ferry · Passenger ferry
Schifffahrtslinie		Shipping route
Naturschutzgebiet · Sperrgebiet		Nature reserve · Prohibited area
Nationalpark · Naturpark · Wald		National park · natural park · Forest
Straße für Kfz. gesperrt	X X X X X	Road closed to motor vehicles
Straße mit Gebühr		Toll road
Straße mit Wintersperre	XII-II	Road closed in winter
Straße für Wohnanhänger gesperrt bzw. nicht empfehlenswert		Road closed or not recommended for caravans
Touristenstraße · Pass	Weinstraße ‿1510	Tourist route · Pass
Schöner Ausblick · Rundblick · Landschaftlich bes. schöne Strecke		Scenic view · Panoramic view · Route with beautiful scenery
Heilbad · Schwimmbad		Spa · Swimming pool
Jugendherberge · Campingplatz	▲ X ⚑	Youth hostel · Camping site
Golfplatz · Sprungschanze		Golf-course · Ski jump
Kirche im Ort, freistehend · Kapelle		Church · Chapel
Kloster · Klosterruine		Monastery · Monastery ruin
Synagoge · Moschee		Synagogue · Mosque
Schloss, Burg · Schloss-, Burgruine		Palace, castle · Ruin
Turm · Funk-, Fernsehturm		Tower · Radio-, TV-tower
Leuchtturm · Kraftwerk		Lighthouse · Power station
Wasserfall · Schleuse		Waterfall · Lock
Bauwerk · Marktplatz, Areal		Important building · Market place, area
Ausgrabungs- u. Ruinenstätte · Bergwerk	⚒	Arch. excavation, ruins · Mine
Dolmen · Menhir · Nuraghen	π Ω ᨒ	Dolmen · Menhir · Nuraghe
Hünen-, Hügelgrab · Soldatenfriedhof	☆	Cairn · Military cemetery
Hotel, Gasthaus, Berghütte · Höhle		Hotel, inn, refuge · Cave

Kultur
Malerisches Ortsbild · Ortshöhe — WIEN (171) — **Culture**
Picturesque town · Elevation

Eine Reise wert — ★★ MILANO — Worth a journey

Lohnt einen Umweg — ★ TEMPLIN — Worth a detour

Sehenswert — Andermatt — Worth seeing

Landschaft
Eine Reise wert — ★★ Las Cañadas — **Landscape**
Worth a journey

Lohnt einen Umweg — ★ Texel — Worth a detour

Sehenswert — Dikti — Worth seeing

MARCO POLO Erlebnistour 1 — **MARCO POLO Discovery Tour 1**

MARCO POLO Erlebnistouren — **MARCO POLO Discovery Tours**

MARCO POLO Highlight — ★ — **MARCO POLO Highlight**

FOR YOUR NEXT TRIP...

MARCO POLO TRAVEL GUIDES

Travel with Insider Tips

INDEX

This index lists all towns, bays, destinations and estates as well as names and keywords featured in this guide. Numbers in bold indicate a main entry.

CREDITS

WRITE TO US

e-mail: info@marcopologuides.co.uk

Did you have a great holiday?
Is there something on your mind?
Whatever it is, let us know!
Whether you want to praise, alert us to errors or give us a personal tip – MARCO POLO would be pleased to hear from you.
We do everything we can to provide the very latest information for your trip.

Nevertheless, despite all of our authors' thorough research, errors can creep in. MARCO POLO does not accept any liability for this. Please contact us by e-mail or post.

MARCO POLO Travel Publishing Ltd
Pinewood, Chineham Business Park
Crockford Lane, Chineham
Basingstoke, Hampshire RG24 8AL
United Kingdom

PICTURE CREDITS

Cover photograph: Cala Macarelleta (Schapowalow/SIME: O. Fantuz)
Images: DuMont Bildarchiv: Schröder (113); f1online/AGE: G. Azumendi (11), R. Campillo (30); Getty Images: Imgorthand (106/107); Getty Images/Westend61 (3); huber-images: G. Croppi (17, 18 centre), R. Schmid (5, 14/15, 20/21, 34, 52/53, 61, 62/63, 67, 74/75, 80/81, 82); F. Ihlow (112 bottom,124/125); laif: M. Amme (89, 102/103), G. Azumendi (37, 73), Huber (54, 110, 112 top), Knechtel (9, 18 top), T. Linkel (10, 29), laif/Le Figaro Magazine: Martin (2, 98); laif/REA: F. Perri (19 bottom, 25, 40); Look: H. Leue (7), K. Maeritz (flap left, 90/91), Richter (flap right); Look/age fotostock (8, 32/33, 56, 64, 76); Look/travelstock44 (4 top, 22); K. Maeritz (78); mauritius images: S. Beuthan (69, 110/111), J. Warburton-Lee (51); mauritius images/age (4 bottom, 26/27, 44, 95); mauritius images/age fotostock: A. Leiva (86), M. Mayol (104/105), mauritius images/Alamy (28 left, 30/31, 31, 38, 47, 70/71, 109), G. B. Evans (43), M. Galan Still (6); mauritius images/Axiom Photographic (85); mauritius images/Cubolmages (28 right); mauritius images/imagebroker: Stella (59); mauritius images/islandspics/Alamy (19 top); mauritius images/Robert Harding (48); mauritius images/Westend61: J. Stock (18 bottom); Schapowalow/SIME: O. Fantuz (1); K. Thiele (111); vario images/Axiom (12/13)

3rd Edition – fully revised and updated 2019

Worldwide Distribution: Marco Polo Travel Publishing Ltd, Pinewood, Chineham Business Park, Crockford Lane, Basingstoke, Hampshire RG24 8AL, United Kingdom. E-mail: sales@marcopolouk.com
© MAIRDUMONT GmbH & Co. KG, Ostfildern
Chief editor: Marion Zorn
Author: Jörg Dörpinghaus, co-author: Izabella Gawin; editor: Karin Liebe, Jochen Schürmann
Programme supervision: Lucas Forst-Gill, Susanne Heimburger, Tamara Hub, Johanna Jiranek, Nikolai Michaelis, Kristin Wittemann, Tim Wohlbold
Picture editors: Gabriele Forst, Stefanie Wiese; What's hot: wunder media, Munich
Cartography road atlas & pull-out map: © MAIRDUMONT, Ostfildern
Design front cover, p. 1, pull-out map cover: Karl Anders – Büro für Visual Stories, Hamburg; interior: milchhof:atelier, Berlin; Discovery Tours, p. 2/3: Susan Chaaban Dipl.-Des. (FH)
Translated from German by Susan Jones; Samantha Riffle
Prepress: writehouse, Cologne; InterMedia, Ratingen
Phrase book in cooperation with Ernst Klett Sprachen GmbH, Stuttgart, Editorial by Pons Wörterbücher

All rights reserved. No part of this book may be reproduced, stored in a retrieval system or transmitted in any form or by any means (electronic, mechanical, photocopying, recording or otherwise) without prior written permission from the publisher. Printed in China

MIX
Paper from responsible sources
FSC® C124385

DOS & DON'TS 👆

Here are a few things to look out for on your Menorca holiday

DO TAKE CARE WHEN SWIMMING

The sea south of Menorca is particularly well-known for strong currents which can be treacherous, especially off the larger, open beaches. Always observe the warning buoys and do not swim out too far. The north of the island can be dangerous when the *tramuntana* is blowing. Observe the red warning flag on the beaches! If it is flying, you're not allowed into the water; yellow means caution; bathing is only allowed when it is green.

DON'T IGNORE JELLYFISH

In recent years, jellyfish have been sighted repeatedly. Especially the Portuguese man-of-war which has a "sail" above water and long tentacles underwater can induce painful, burning stings and even a shock. Therefore, please pay attention to the flags on the beach: If you see one with a medusa-head on it, better stay out of the water. If on the natural beach you see a washed-up jellyfish, you should also abstain from bathing. If you've been hurt by a jellyfish: Rinse the affected skin parts carefully with seawater and buy an ointment at the pharmacy.

DON'T CLIMB OVER WALLS

Not every Menorcan is happy to see strangers walking across his property. Occasionally a shot gun has even been drawn, more often the dogs are let loose. This is why you absolutely must speak to the owner before setting off on a hike or looking for somewhere to camp "rough". On marked hiking trails, always make sure you close the gate behind you as you cross private property.

DON'T GO INTO TOWN ON SUNDAYS

On Sundays, there's nothing going on in Ciutadella or Maó, because that's when the locals go to the beach and almost all museums, sights and shops are closed. If you want to experience the Mediterranean way of life, better come on another day.

DO BE WARY OF FLOWER GIRLS

In addition to the well-known shell game players, "flower girls" also operate in the tourist resorts in summer. They try to offer flowers to holidaymakers who in turn – disarmed by such kindness – quite often take out their purse or wallet. This opportunity is used by the flower girls to help themselves in the confusion or in the tourists' eagerness to communicate. It is far better to avoid the "friendly" girls in the first place or, if they are being particularly insistent, shout loudly for the police (*policia!*).

DO SAVE WATER

The water table on Menorca has sunk alarmingly in recent years and many wells are already contaminated by salt. As a tourist you too can help save water by using tap water sparingly.